# Minnesota DMV Exam Workbook:

*Your Essential Guide to the Minnesota Driving Test*

**Master the Minnesota DMV Exam with the Best Minnesota Driver's Practice Tests**

# Introduction

Driving is a crucial aspect of daily life in Minnesota, and navigating the roads safely and confidently is essential for both new and experienced drivers. If you are preparing to take your Minnesota driving test, you are likely feeling a mix of excitement and nerves. You may wonder what to expect on the test and how to prepare best to pass it on the first try.

In this book, we provide you with everything you need to know about the Minnesota practice driving test We will cover the different types of driving tests offered in Minnesota, the process for obtaining a driver's license, and the requirements you must meet to be eligible for a license.

We will also delve into the rules of the road and safety measures you should be aware of as a driver in Minnesota.

We understand that preparing for the driving test can be stressful, so we have included a wealth of information and resources to help you feel more confident and prepared on test day. We will provide tips and strategies for improving your driving skills and increasing your chances of passing the test.

We will also provide practice test questions and sample scenarios to better understand what to expect on the test.

But the goal of this book is not just to help you pass the driving test. Our ultimate aim is to help you become a responsible and safe driver. Driving is a privilege that comes with great responsibility, and we want to empower you with the knowledge and skills necessary to navigate the roads confidently and with care.

So whether you are a first-time driver looking to obtain your license or an experienced driver seeking to refresh your knowledge of Minnesota driving laws, this book is for you. We hope it serves as a valuable resource as you prepare for your driving test and embark on your journey as a licensed driver in Minnesota.

# Table of Contents

*This includes knowledge of the various parts of a vehicle and how to properly maintain them, as well as knowledge of how to safely load and unload a vehicle.*

*This includes information about how to safely share the road with other vehicles, pedestrians, and bicycles.*

*This includes knowledge of how to handle various types of emergencies that may occur while driving, such as blowouts, fires, and collisions.*

*This includes knowledge of the size and weight limits for vehicles on Minnesota roads, as well as the rules for towing.*

*This includes information about the various types of public transportation available in Minnesota, as well as the rules for using them.*

# Traffic laws and signs

Welcome to Chapter 1 of the Minnesota DMV Exam Workbook, where we embark on an exciting journey through the traffic laws and road signs that govern the Land of 10,000 Lakes. In this chapter, we will delve into the fundamental knowledge necessary for becoming a safe and responsible driver in Minnesota. Understanding and adhering to traffic laws and effectively interpreting road signs are crucial skills that will not only help you pass your DMV exam but also ensure your safety and the safety of others on the road.

Traffic laws are the backbone of safe and efficient transportation. They provide structure, order, and predictability, enabling motorists to navigate the roads in a coordinated and harmonious manner. This section will emphasize the significance of traffic laws in promoting safety, minimizing accidents, and maintaining a smooth flow of traffic. By familiarizing yourself with these laws, you will be equipped to make informed decisions and drive responsibly.

## Sources of Traffic Laws

This section will explore the various sources of traffic laws in Minnesota. From state statutes to local ordinances, understanding where traffic laws originate will give you insight into the hierarchical structure of these regulations. We will also touch upon how traffic laws can evolve over time to accommodate changing circumstances and address emerging issues.

## Common Traffic Violations

This section will highlight some of the most common traffic violations committed by drivers in Minnesota. Understanding these violations and their associated penalties will help you avoid legal consequences and promote responsible driving behavior. We will cover offenses such as speeding, running red lights or stop signs, improper lane usage, and distracted driving.

**Right-of-Way Rules**

Right-of-way rules establish the order in which vehicles and pedestrians have the legal right to proceed at intersections and other points of conflict on the road. This section will provide a comprehensive overview of right-of-way rules in Minnesota, including scenarios involving yield signs, stop signs, traffic signals, and uncontrolled intersections. Understanding and respecting right-of-way rules are vital for preventing accidents and ensuring the smooth flow of traffic.

**Minnesota Road Signs**

Road signs are an essential communication tool on the roadways. They provide valuable information, warnings, and instructions to drivers, cyclists, and pedestrians. In this section, we will explore the different types of road signs in Minnesota, including regulatory signs, warning signs, and guide signs. We will discuss their shapes, colors, and symbols, as well as their specific meanings and implications.

**Understanding Traffic Signals**

Traffic signals are an integral part of the transportation system, controlling the flow of vehicles and pedestrians at intersections. This section will provide a detailed examination of traffic signals in Minnesota, including the meanings of different signal colors, the purpose of arrows, and the importance of understanding and obeying signal indications. We will also discuss scenarios involving flashing signals, pedestrian signals, and railroad crossings.

**Work Zones and Special Traffic Situations**

Work zones and special traffic situations require extra caution and attention from drivers. This section will address the challenges and responsibilities associated with driving through work zones, school zones, and construction areas. Understanding the importance of reduced speed limits, following flagger instructions, and maintaining vigilance in these situations is crucial for the safety of road workers, pedestrians, and yourself.

## Study Strategies for Traffic Laws and Signs

To effectively prepare for the Minnesota DMV exam, it is important to implement study strategies specific to traffic laws and signs. This section will provide you with practical tips for studying the material, such as using flashcards, taking practice tests, and familiarizing yourself with the Minnesota Driver's Manual. We will also emphasize the significance of situational awareness and real-life application of traffic laws and road signs.

As we progress through the subsequent chapters of this workbook, the knowledge gained from understanding Minnesota's traffic laws and road signs will serve as a strong foundation for your overall driver education. So, let's dive into the fascinating world of traffic laws and signs, acquiring the necessary skills to become a safe, responsible, and law-abiding driver in Minnesota.

For training purposes, you can mark the ▢ symbol next to what you think is the correct answer: Once you have chosen the correct answer, use a pencil or pen to mark the ▢ symbol next to that answer.

# Traffic laws and signs exam

**1.  What does a red octagonal sign with white letters "STOP" indicate?**

A.  ▢ Proceed with caution

B.  ▢ Slow down

C.  ▢ Stop completely

D.  ▢ Merge with traffic

**2. What does a yellow diamond-shaped sign with black symbols "YIELD" mean?**

A.  ▢ Speed up and proceed

B.  ▢ Slow down and proceed with caution

C.  ▢ Stop and wait for oncoming traffic

D.  ▢ Yield the right-of-way to other vehicles

**3. What does a rectangular white sign with black letters "SPEED LIMIT 55" represent?**

A.  ▢ Recommended speed for the road

B.  ▢ Minimum speed required

C.  ▢ Maximum speed allowed

D.  ▢ Average speed of other vehicles

**4. What does a round blue sign with a white arrow indicate?**

A.  ▢ One-way street

B.  ▢ School zone ahead

C.  ▢ Pedestrian crossing

D.  ▢ Mandatory direction of travel

**5. What does a red triangle-shaped sign with white letters "YIELD AHEAD" mean?**

A.  ▢ Proceed without stopping

B.  ▢ Merge with traffic

C.  ▢ Slow down and prepare to yield

D.  ▢ Stop and wait for oncoming traffic

**6.  What does a white rectangular sign with black symbols "NO LEFT TURN" represent?**

A.  ▢ Left turn is allowed

B.  ▢ Left turn is prohibited

C.  ▢ Left turn is mandatory

D.  ▢ Left turn is optional

**7. What does a yellow circular sign with a black cross indicate?**

A.  ▢ Railroad crossing ahead

B.  ▢ Hospital ahead

C.  ▢ No parking zone

D.  ▢ Intersection ahead

**8. What does a red and white triangular sign with an exclamation mark indicate?**

A.  ▢ Road work ahead

B.  ▢ No passing zone

C.  ▢ Sharp turn ahead

D.  ▢ Warning of a potential hazard

**9. What does a rectangular orange sign with black symbols "ROAD WORK AHEAD" mean?**

A. ▢ Detour ahead

B. ▢ No entry

C. ▢ Construction zone ahead

D. ▢ End of work zone

**10. What does a rectangular green sign with white letters "EXIT 25" represent?**

A. ▢ Highway exit number

B. ▢ Entry point to a city

C. ▢ Rest area ahead

D. ▢ Speed limit for the upcoming exit

**11. What does a red circle with a white horizontal line indicate?**

A. ▢ No stopping

B. ▢ No left turn

C. ▢ No entry

D. ▢ No parking

**12. What does a yellow diamond-shaped sign with two black arrows pointing in opposite directions represent?**

A. ▢ Divided highway begins

B. ▢ Two-way traffic ahead

C. ▢ U-turn permitted

D. ▢ Road narrows ahead

**13. What does a rectangular white sign with a black bicycle symbol indicate?**

A. ☐ Bicycle parking area

B. ☐ Bicycle crossing

C. ☐ Bicycle lane

D. ☐ Bicycle prohibited


**14. What does a rectangular orange sign with black symbols "WORKERS AHEAD" mean?**

A. ☐ Workers' union meeting point

B. ☐ Reduced speed zone

C. ☐ Road workers present

D. ☐ Road maintenance in progress


**15. What does a round yellow sign with a black X-shaped symbol indicate?**

A. ☐ No U-turn

B. ☐ No right turn

C. ☐ No left turn

D. ☐ No passing

# Correct answers for traffic laws and signs exam

1. **C**. Stop completely
2. **D**. Yield the right-of-way to other vehicles
3. **C**. Maximum speed allowed
4. **D**. Mandatory direction of travel
5. **C**. Slow down and prepare to yield
6. **B**. Left turn is prohibited
7. **A**. Railroad crossing ahead
8. **D**. Warning of a potential hazard
9. **C**. Construction zone ahead
10. **A**. Highway exit number
11. **C**. No entry
12. **B**. Two-way traffic ahead
13. **C**. Bicycle lane
14. **C**. Road workers present
15. **A**. No U-turn

# Traffic laws and signs exam 2

**1. What does a white sign with a red circle and a red line through it indicate?**

A. ▢ No entry

B. ▢ No U-turn

C. ▢ No parking

D. ▢ No passing

**2. What does a yellow sign with a black crossed-out arrow pointing left indicate?**

A. ▢ No left turn

B. ▢ No U-turn

C. ▢ No right turn

D. ▢ No passing zone

**3. What does a rectangular orange sign with black symbols of workers indicate?**

A. ▢ Construction zone

B. ▢ School zone

C. ▢ Hospital zone

D. ▢ No passing zone

**4. What does a white sign with a black bicycle symbol indicate?**

A. ▢ Bicycle crossing

B. ▢ Bike lane ahead

C. ▢ Bike parking

D. ▢ Share the road with bicycles

**5. What does a blue sign with a white car symbol indicate?**

A. ▢ Parking lot ahead

B. ▢ Car wash

C. ▢ Car rental service

D. ▢ Rest area for vehicles

**6. What does a yellow sign with a black pedestrian symbol indicate?**

A. ▢ Pedestrian crossing

B. ▢ School zone

C. ▢ Hospital zone

D. ▢ No pedestrians allowed

**7. What does a white sign with a black truck symbol indicate?**

A. ▢ Truck stop ahead

B. ▢ No trucks allowed

C. ▢ Truck weigh station ahead

D. ▢ Truck parking area

**8. What does a blue sign with a white airplane symbol indicate?**

A. ▢ Airport ahead

B. ▢ No flying zone

C. ▢ Landing strip ahead

D. ▢ Airplane parking area

**9. What does a white sign with a red circle and a white number indicate?**

A. ▢ Speed limit

B. ▢ Distance to the next exit

C. ▢ Lane closure ahead

D. ▢ Road closure ahead

**10. What does a white sign with a black dollar symbol indicate?**

A. ▢ Toll booth ahead

B. ▢ No cash payment

C. ▢ Rest area with ATMs

D. ▢ Financial district ahead


**11. What does a blue sign with a white "i" symbol indicate?**

A. ▢ Information center ahead

B. ▢ Intersection ahead

C. ▢ Interstate highway entrance

D. ▢ Emergency hospital ahead


**12. What does a white sign with a black arrow pointing upward indicate?**

A. ▢ One-way street ahead

B. ▢ Exit only ahead

C. ▢ Pedestrian crossing

D. ▢ Hospital zone

**13. What does a yellow sign with a black drawing of a deer indicate?**

A. ▢ Wildlife crossing

B. ▢ No hunting zone

C. ▢ Deer farm ahead

D. ▢ No deer allowed

**14. What does a red sign with white letters "RR" indicate?**

A. ▢ Railroad crossing ahead

B. ▢ Road repair ahead

C. ▢ Restricted road

D. ▢ Right of way

**15. What does a white sign with a red circle and a white hand symbol indicate?**

A. ▢ Yield to pedestrians

B. ▢ No hand gestures allowed

C. ▢ High-five zone

D. ▢ Handicap parking ahead

# Correct answers to traffic laws and signs exam 2

1. **A**. No entry
2. **B**. No left turn
3. **A**. Construction zone
4. **D**. Share the road with bicycles
5. **D**. Rest area for vehicles
6. **A**. Pedestrian crossing
7. **C**. Truck weigh station ahead
8. **A**. Airport ahead
9. **A**. Speed limit
10. **C**. Rest area with ATMs
11. **A**. Information center ahead
12. **A**. One-way street ahead
13. **A**. Wildlife crossing
14. **A**. Railroad crossing ahead
15. **A**. Yield to pedestrians

# Traffic Laws and signs exam 3

**1. What does a red sign with a white hand symbol indicate?**

A. ▢ Yield to pedestrians

B. ▢ No hand gestures allowed

C. ▢ High-five zone

D. ▢ Handicap parking ahead

**2. What does a white sign with a black arrow pointing downward indicate?**

A. ▢ One-way street ahead

B. ▢ No entry

C. ▢ Exit only ahead

D. ▢ Hospital zone

**3. What does a yellow sign with a black drawing of a bicycle indicate?**

A. ▢ Bicycle crossing

B. ▢ No bicycles allowed

C. ▢ Bike rental shop ahead

D. ▢ Share the road with bicycles

**4. What does a white sign with a red circle and a white cross indicate?**

A. ▫ Intersection ahead

B. ▫ Hospital zone

C. ▫ Emergency stop area ahead

D. ▫ No right turn


**5. What does a blue sign with a white ship symbol indicate?**

A. ▫ Port ahead

B. ▫ No sailing zone

C. ▫ Boat rental service

D. ▫ Marina ahead


**6. What does a yellow sign with a black drawing of a school bus indicate?**

A. ▫ School zone

B. ▫ School bus stop ahead

C. ▫ School bus parking area

D. ▫ No school buses allowed

**7. What does a white sign with a black drawing of a gas pump indicate?**

A. ▢ Gas station ahead

B. ▢ No fueling zone

C. ▢ Fuel station for government vehicles

D. ▢ Fuel quality testing area

**8. What does a blue sign with a white wheelchair symbol indicate?**

A. ▢ Disabled parking ahead

B. ▢ Wheelchair rental service

C. ▢ Handicap-accessible restroom

D. ▢ Wheelchair crossing zone

**9. What does a white sign with a black drawing of a deer and an arrow indicate?**

A. ▢ Deer crossing

B. ▢ Deer hunting zone

C. ▢ Deer farm ahead

D. ▢ No deer allowed

**10. What does a red sign with white letters "STOP" indicate?**

A. ▢ Stop sign ahead

B. ▢ Intersection ahead

C. ▢ Restricted road

D. ▢ Road repair ahead

**11. What does a white sign with a black arrow pointing to the right indicate?**

A. ▢ Right turn only

B. ▢ No right turn

C. ▢ Roundabout ahead

D. ▢ Detour to the right

**12. What does a yellow sign with a black drawing of a construction worker indicate?**

A. ▢ Construction zone

B. ▢ Construction worker's residence ahead

C. ▢ Construction worker crossing

D. ▢ No construction vehicles allowed

**13. What does a white sign with a black drawing of a person running indicate?**

A. ▢ Marathon event ahead

B. ▢ No running allowed

C. ▢ Jogging trail ahead

D. ▢ Pedestrian activity zone

**14. What does a green sign with white letters "EXIT" indicate?**

A. ▢ Exit ahead

B. ▢ Entrance to highway

C. ▢ Emergency exit ahead

D. ▢ No exits for next 10 miles

**15. What does a white sign with a black drawing of a car on an inclined road indicate?**

A. ▢ Steep hill ahead

B. ▢ No parking on hills

C. ▢ Car racing zone ahead

D. ▢ Car wash ahead

## Correct answers for traffic laws and signs exam 3

1.  **A**. Yield to pedestrians
2.  **C**. Exit only ahead
3.  **D**. Share the road with bicycles
4.  **B**. Hospital zone
5.  **A**. Port ahead
6.  **B**. School bus stop ahead
7.  **A**. Gas station ahead
8.  **A**. Disabled parking ahead
9.  **A**. Deer crossing
10. **A**. Stop sign ahead
11. **A**. Right turn only
12. **A**. Construction zone
13. **D**. Pedestrian activity zone
14. **A**. Exit ahead
15. **A**. Steep hill ahead

# Traffic laws and signs exam 4

**1. What does a white sign with a black drawing of a person walking indicate?**

A. ▢ Pedestrian crossing

B. ▢ No walking allowed

C. ▢ Walking trail ahead

D. ▢ Walking competition zone


**2. What does a yellow sign with a black drawing of a truck tipping over indicate?**

A. ▢ Truck rollover zone

B. ▢ No trucks allowed

C. ▢ Truck parking area

D. ▢ Truck weigh station ahead


**3. What does a white sign with a black drawing of a train indicate?**

A. ▢ Railroad crossing ahead

B. ▢ No trains allowed

C. ▢ Train station ahead

D. ▢ Train repair zone

**4. What does a red sign with a white cross indicate?**

A. ▢ First aid station ahead

B. ▢ No stopping zone

C. ▢ Hospital zone

D. ▢ Crosswalk ahead

**5. What does a blue sign with a white drawing of an airplane indicate?**

A. ▢ Airport ahead

B. ▢ No flying zone

C. ▢ Airplane rental service

D. ▢ Airshow ahead

**6. What does a yellow sign with a black drawing of a person on a bicycle indicate?**

A. ▢ Bike path ahead

B. ▢ No bicycles allowed

C. ▢ Bicycle repair shop ahead

D. ▢ Bicycle race zone

**7. What does a white sign with a black drawing of a fuel nozzle indicate?**

A. ▫ Gas station ahead

B. ▫ No fueling zone

C. ▫ Fuel station for commercial vehicles

D. ▫ Fuel efficiency testing area

**8. What does a green sign with white letters "HOSPITAL" indicate?**

A. ▫ Hospital ahead

B. ▫ Nursing home ahead C

C. ▫ Hospital zone

D. ▫ No hospital services available

**9. What does a white sign with a black drawing of a school building indicate?**

A. ▫ School zone

B. ▫ School ahead

C. ▫ School bus stop ahead

D. ▫ School crossing zone

**10. What does a yellow sign with a black drawing of a construction cone indicate?**

A. ▢ Construction zone ahead

B. ▢ No construction vehicles allowed

C. ▢ Construction workers' break area

D. ▢ Construction cone store ahead

**11. What does a white sign with a black drawing of a person riding a horse indicate?**

A. ▢ Equestrian crossing

B. ▢ No horses allowed

C. ▢ Horse racing track ahead

D. ▢ Horseback riding trail ahead

**12. What does a red sign with a white drawing of a person on a bicycle indicate?**

A. ▢ Bike lane ahead

B. ▢ No bicycles allowed

C. ▢ Bike rental service

D. ▢ Bike race zone

**13. What does a white sign with a black drawing of a truck indicate?**

A. ▢ Truck route ahead

B. ▢ No trucks allowed

C. ▢ Truck weigh station ahead

D. ▢ Truck repair zone

**14. What does a yellow sign with a black drawing of a person with a flag indicate?**

A. ▢ Construction zone with flagger ahead

B. ▢ No flagging allowed

C. ▢ Flag football field ahead

D. ▢ Flagpole ahead

**15. What does a blue sign with white letters "P" indicate?**

A. ▢ Parking area ahead

B. ▢ No parking zone

C. ▢ Pedestrian crossing zone

D. ▢ Parking for police vehicles only

# Correct answers for traffic laws and signs exam 4

1. **A**. Pedestrian crossing

2. **A**. Truck rollover zone

3. **A**. Railroad crossing ahead

4. **A**. First aid station ahead

5. **A**. Airport ahead

6. **A**. Bike path ahead

7. **A**. Gas station ahead

8. **A**. Hospital ahead

9. **B**. School ahead

10. **A**. Construction zone ahead

11. **A**. Equestrian crossing

12. **B**. No bicycles allowed

13. **A**. Truck route ahead

14. **A**. Construction zone with flagger ahead

15. **A**. Parking area ahead

# Traffic laws and signs exam 5

**1.  What does a white sign with a black drawing of a camera indicate?**

A. ▢ Speed enforcement zone

B. ▢ No photography zone

C. ▢ Traffic surveillance ahead

D. ▢ Camera store ahead

**2.  What does a yellow sign with a black drawing of a flag person indicate?**

A. ▢ Construction zone with flagger ahead

B. ▢ No flagging zone

C. ▢ Flag football field ahead

D. ▢ Flag store ahead

**3.  What does a white sign with a black drawing of a house indicate?**

A. ▢ Residential area ahead

B. ▢ No housing zone

C. ▢ House construction zone

D. ▢ House museum ahead

4. **What does a red sign with a white drawing of a fire hydrant indicate?**

A. ▢ Fire hydrant zone

B. ▢ No parking zone

C. ▢ Fire station ahead

D. ▢ Fireworks store ahead

5. **What does a blue sign with white letters "REST AREA" indicate?**

A. ▢ Rest area ahead

B. ▢ No resting zone

C. ▢ Restaurant ahead

D. ▢ Restricted access zone

6. **What does a yellow sign with a black drawing of a dog indicate?**

A. ▢ Watch for animals ahead

B. ▢ No pets allowed

C. ▢ Dog park ahead

D. ▢ Pet store ahead

**7. What does a white sign with a black drawing of a person skiing indicate?**

A. ▢ Ski resort ahead

B. ▢ No skiing allowed

C. ▢ Ski shop ahead

D. ▢ Slippery road ahead

**8. What does a green sign with white letters "PLAYGROUND" indicate?**

A. ▢ Playground ahead

B. ▢ No playing allowed

C. ▢ Sports complex ahead

D. ▢ Children's museum ahead

**9. What does a white sign with a black drawing of a helicopter indicate?**

A. ▢ Heliport ahead

B. ▢ No helicopters allowed

C. ▢ Helicopter tour service

D. ▢ Helicopter landing zone

**10. What does a yellow sign with a black drawing of a flag indicating "SLOW" indicate?**

A. ▢ Reduced speed zone

B. ▢ No flagging allowed

C. ▢ Slow vehicle ahead

D. ▢ Flag store ahead

**11. What does a white sign with a black drawing of a person with a cane indicate?**

A. ▢ Pedestrian crosswalk for the visually impaired

B. ▢ No walking allowed

C. ▢ Walking cane store ahead

D. ▢ Walking tour ahead

**12. What does a red sign with a white drawing of a hand making a "stop" gesture indicate?**

A. ▢ Stop for pedestrians

B. ▢ No hand gestures allowed

C. ▢ Stop sign ahead

D. ▢ Hand massage parlor ahead

**13. What does a white sign with a black drawing of a person with a hard hat indicate?**

A. ▢ Construction zone ahead

B. ▢ No hard hats allowed

C. ▢ Construction worker crossing

D. ▢ Construction equipment rental ahead

**14. What does a yellow sign with a black drawing of a bicycle and an arrow indicate?**

A. ▢ Bicycle route ahead

B. ▢ No bicycles allowed

C. ▢ Bike rental service

D. ▢ Bicycle race zone

**15. What does a blue sign with white letters "TRUCKS" indicate?**

A. ▢ Truck route ahead

B. ▢ No trucks allowed

C. ▢ Truck stop ahead

D. ▢ Truck repair zone

# Correct answers for traffic laws and signs exam 5

1. **A**. Speed enforcement zone

2. **A**. Construction zone with flagger ahead

3. **A**. Residential area ahead

4. **B**. No parking zone

5. **A**. Rest area ahead

6. **A**. Watch for animals ahead

7. **D**. Slippery road ahead

8. **A**. Playground ahead

9. **A**. Heliport ahead

10. **C**. Slow vehicle ahead

11. **A**. Pedestrian crosswalk for the visually impaired

12. **A**. Stop for pedestrians

13. **C**. Construction worker crossing

14. **A**. Bicycle route ahead

15. **B**. No trucks allowed

# Vehicle control and safety

Welcome to Chapter 2 of the Minnesota DMV Exam Workbook, where we explore the critical aspects of vehicle control and safety. In this chapter, we will delve into the skills and knowledge necessary to operate a vehicle with precision, confidence, and utmost safety. Understanding the principles of vehicle control and implementing proper safety measures are key factors in becoming a responsible driver on Minnesota's roads.

-Vehicle control is the foundation of safe and effective driving. This section will emphasize the significance of mastering vehicle control skills, such as steering, accelerating, and braking. We will discuss the direct correlation between proper vehicle control and the ability to respond to different driving scenarios, navigate hazards, and maintain control of the vehicle at all times.

As we progress through this chapter, remember that vehicle control and safety go hand in hand. By mastering the skills and concepts covered, you will be well-equipped to handle various driving situations with confidence and responsibility. So, let's dive into the details and explore the world of vehicle control and safety, unlocking the keys to becoming a competent and safe driver in Minnesota.

For training purposes, you can mark the ▢ symbol next to what you think is the correct answer: Once you have chosen the correct answer, use a pencil or pen to mark the ▢ symbol next to that answer.

# Vehicle control and safety exam

1. **What should you do if your vehicle starts to skid?**

A. ▢ Slam on the brakes

B. ▢ Steer in the opposite direction of the skid

C. ▢ Maintain your current steering input

D. ▢ Accelerate to regain control

2. **When should you use your turn signals**

A. ▢ Only when changing lanes

B. ▢ Only when turning right

C. ▢ Only when turning left

D. ▢ When changing lanes or turning

3. **What is the purpose of an anti-lock braking system (ABS)?**

A. ▢ To increase fuel efficiency

B. ▢ To prevent tire blowouts

C. ▢ To improve steering control during hard braking

D. ▢ To reduce engine noise

4. **What is the recommended following distance in ideal driving conditions?**

A. ▢ 1 second

B. ▢ 2 seconds

C. ▢ 3 seconds

D. ▢ 4 seconds

5. **When should you use your high beam headlights?**

A. ▢ In heavy traffic

B. ▢ In foggy conditions

C. ▢ In well-lit areas

D. ▢ When driving at night in open areas

6. **What should you do if your vehicle's tire blows out?**

A. ▢ Slam on the brakes

B. ▢ Accelerate to maintain control

C. ▢ Steer sharply in the opposite direction

D. ▢ Gradually release the accelerator and steer to a safe location

7. **What is the purpose of the blind spot mirrors on your vehicle's side mirrors?**

A. ▢ To enhance the vehicle's aesthetics

B. ▢ To provide a wider field of vision

C. ▢ To reduce wind resistance

D. ▢ To eliminate blind spots completely

8. **When parking on a hill with a curb, which way should you turn your wheels?**

A. ▢ Away from the curb

B. ▢ Towards the curb

C. ▢ It doesn't matter

D. ▢ Turn the wheels in the opposite direction of the hill's slope

9. **What is the proper hand position on the steering wheel?**

A. ▢ 9 o'clock and 3 o'clock

B. ▢ 10 o'clock and 2 o'clock

C. ▢ 12 o'clock and 6 o'clock

D. ▢ 11 o'clock and 5 o'clock

**10. When should you adjust your rearview mirror to the night driving position?**

A. ▢ When it's raining

B. ▢ When there's heavy traffic

C. ▢ When driving during the day

D. ▢ When you see glare from the headlights of vehicles behind you

**11. What should you do if your vehicle's accelerator becomes stuck?**

A. ▢ Pump the brakes repeatedly

B. ▢ Shift into neutral

C. ▢ Turn off the ignition

D. ▢ Steer into oncoming traffic

**12. What does a flashing yellow traffic signal indicate?**

A. ▢ Stop and proceed with caution

B. ▢ Prepare to yield to oncoming traffic

C. ▢ Proceed without stopping

D. ▢ Stop and wait for a green signal

**13. What should you do if your vehicle's brakes fail?**

A. ▢ Slam on the brakes repeatedly

B. ▢ Shift into a lower gear

C. ▢ Engage the parking brake

D. ▢ Pump the brakes rapidly

**14. What is the primary purpose of wearing a seat belt?**

A. ▢ To keep you comfortable while driving

B. ▢ To enhance your vehicle's safety features

C. ▢ To prevent you from being ejected in a crash

D. ▢ To avoid getting a traffic citation

**15. What should you do if your vehicle starts to hydroplane on wet roads?**

A. ▢ Slam on the brakes

B. ▢ Accelerate to regain control

C. ▢ Steer sharply in the opposite direction

D. ▢ Gradually release the accelerator and steer straight

# Correct answers for vehicle control and safety exam

1. **B**. Steer in the opposite direction of the skid

2. **D**. When changing lanes or turning

3. **C**. To improve steering control during hard braking

4. **C**. 3 seconds

5. **D**. When driving at night in open areas

6. **D**. Gradually release the accelerator and steer to a safe location

7. **B**. To provide a wider field of vision

8. **B**. Towards the curb

9. **B**. 10 o'clock and 2 o'clock

10. **D**. When you see glare from the headlights of vehicles behind you

11. **B**. Shift into neutral

12. **C**. Proceed without stopping

13. **D**. Pump the brakes rapidly

14. **C**. To prevent you from being ejected in a crash

15. **D**. Gradually release the accelerator and steer straight

# Vehicle control and safety exam 2

1.  **What should you do if your vehicle's headlights suddenly fail while driving at night?**

A. ▢ Immediately stop in the middle of the road

B. ▢ Keep driving, relying on the streetlights

C. ▢ Turn on your hazard lights and pull off the road

D. ▢ Flash your high beam headlights to see the road ahead

2.  **When should you use your hazard lights while driving?**

A. ▢ When you are lost and need directions

B. ▢ When you want to park illegally for a short time

C. ▢ When your vehicle has broken down or is in a hazardous location

D. ▢ When you are driving in heavy traffic and want to warn other drivers

3.  **What should you do if you experience a sudden tire blowout while driving?**

A. ▢ Slam on the brakes and steer sharply

B. ▢ Accelerate to maintain control of the vehicle

C. ▢ Gradually release the accelerator and maintain a firm grip on the steering wheel

D. ▢ Immediately pull over to the side of the road and inspect the tire

**4. What does it mean if your vehicle's dashboard warning light for the engine is illuminated?**

A. ▢ Your vehicle is low on fuel

B. ▢ The engine temperature is too high

C. ▢ The engine is experiencing a malfunction

D. ▢ Your vehicle's oil level is low

**5. When should you use your fog lights while driving?**

A. ▢ In clear weather conditions during the day

B. ▢ Only during foggy or misty weather conditions

C. ▢ When driving at night on well-lit roads

D. ▢ Whenever you feel like it

**6. What is the purpose of the side view mirrors on your vehicle?**

A. ▢ To enhance the vehicle's aesthetics

B. ▢ To provide a clear view of the road ahead

C. ▢ To eliminate blind spots completely

D. ▢ To monitor the surrounding traffic while driving

**7. What should you do if you encounter a vehicle approaching you with its high beams on?**

A. ▢ Flash your high beams back at them

B. ▢ Keep your low beams on and look to the right side of the road

C. ▢ Slow down and maintain your current driving speed

D. ▢ Look to the right side of the road and use the lane markings as a guide

**8. What is the purpose of the vehicle's suspension system?**

A. ▢ To improve fuel efficiency

B. ▢ To enhance the vehicle's aerodynamics

C. ▢ To provide a smooth and comfortable ride

D. ▢ To reduce engine noise and vibrations

**9. What should you do if you approach a traffic signal that is not working?**

A. ▢ Treat it as a stop sign and proceed with caution

B. ▢ Ignore it and proceed through the intersection

C. ▢ Drive at increased speed to clear the intersection quickly

D. ▢ Honk your horn and proceed through the intersection

**10. What should you do if your vehicle's accelerator becomes stuck?**

A. ▢ Slam on the brakes repeatedly

B. ▢ Shift into neutral

C. ▢ Turn off the ignition

D. ▢ Steer into oncoming traffic

**11. What does a flashing yellow traffic signal indicate?**

A. ▢ Stop and proceed with caution

B. ▢ Prepare to yield to oncoming traffic

C. ▢ Proceed without stopping

D. ▢ Stop and wait for a green signal

**12. What should you do if your vehicle's brakes fail?**

A. ▢ Slam on the brakes repeatedly

B. ▢ Shift into a lower gear

C. ▢ Engage the parking brake

D. ▢ Pump the brakes rapidly

**13. What is the primary purpose of wearing a seat belt?**

A. ▢ To keep you comfortable while driving

B. ▢ To enhance your vehicle's safety features

C. ▢ To prevent you from being ejected in a crash

D. ▢ To avoid getting a traffic citation

## 14. What should you do if your vehicle starts to hydroplane on wet roads?

A. ▢ Slam on the brakes

B. ▢ Accelerate to regain control

C. ▢ Steer sharply in the opposite direction

D. ▢ Gradually release the accelerator and steer straight

## 15. What is the purpose of the catalytic converter in a vehicle's exhaust system?

A. ▢ To increase fuel efficiency

B. ▢ To enhance engine performance

C. ▢ To reduce harmful emissions

D. ▢ To control vehicle noise

# Correct answers for vehicle control and safety exam 2

1.  **C**. Turn on your hazard lights and pull off the road

2.  **C**. When your vehicle has broken down or is in a hazardous location

3.  **C**. Gradually release the accelerator and maintain a firm grip on the steering wheel

4.  **C**. The engine is experiencing a malfunction

5.  **B**. Only during foggy or misty weather conditions

6.  **D**. To monitor the surrounding traffic while driving

7.  **B**. Keep your low beams on and look to the right side of the road

8.  **C**. To provide a smooth and comfortable ride

9.  **A**. Treat it as a stop sign and proceed with caution

10. **B**. Shift into neutral

11. **C**. Proceed without stopping

12. **D**. Pump the brakes rapidly

13. **C**. To prevent you from being ejected in a crash

14. **D**. Gradually release the accelerator and steer straight

15. **C**. To reduce harmful emissions

# Vehicle control and safety exam 3

1.  **What should you do if you encounter a flashing red traffic signal?**

    A. ▢ Proceed without stopping

    B. ▢ Treat it as a stop sign

    C. ▢ Slow down and proceed with caution

    D. ▢ Yield to oncoming traffic

2.  **When should you use your hazard lights while driving?**

    A. ▢ When you want to park illegally for a short time

    B. ▢ When driving in heavy rain or snow

    C. ▢ When you are driving faster than the speed limit

    D. ▢ When you are approaching a green traffic signal

3.  **What should you do if your vehicle's accelerator becomes stuck?**

    A. ▢ Slam on the brakes repeatedly

    B. ▢ Shift into neutral

    C. ▢ Turn off the ignition

    D. ▢ Steer into oncoming traffic

4. **What does a solid yellow traffic signal indicate?**

    A. ▢ Stop and wait for a green signal

    B. ▢ Prepare to yield to oncoming traffic

    C. ▢ Proceed with caution

    D. ▢ Stop and proceed only if it is safe

**5. When should you use your fog lights while driving?**

A. ▢ In clear weather conditions during the day

B. ▢ Only during foggy or misty weather conditions

C. ▢ When driving on a well-lit highway

D. ▢ Whenever you feel like it


**6. What is the purpose of the side view mirrors on your vehicle?**

A. ▢ To enhance the vehicle's aesthetics

B. ▢ To provide a wider field of vision

C. ▢ To eliminate blind spots completely

D. ▢ To reduce wind resistance


**7. What should you do if you encounter a vehicle approaching you with its high beams on?**

A. ▢ Flash your high beams back at them

B. ▢ Keep your low beams on and look to the right side of the road

C. ▢ Slow down and maintain your current driving speed

D. ▢ Look to the right side of the road and use the lane markings as a guide


**8. What is the purpose of the vehicle's suspension system?**

A. ▢ To improve fuel efficiency

B. ▢ To enhance the vehicle's aerodynamics

C. ▢ To provide a smooth and comfortable ride

D. ▢ To reduce engine noise and vibrations

**9. What should you do if you approach a traffic signal that is not working?**

A. ▢ Treat it as a stop sign and proceed with caution

B. ▢ Ignore it and proceed through the intersection

C. ▢ Drive at increased speed to clear the intersection quickly

D. ▢ Honk your horn and proceed through the intersection

**10. What should you do if your vehicle's accelerator becomes stuck?**

A. ▢ Slam on the brakes repeatedly

B. ▢ Shift into neutral

C. ▢ Turn off the ignition

D. ▢ Steer into oncoming traffic

**11. What does a flashing yellow traffic signal indicate?**

A. ▢ Stop and proceed with caution

B. ▢ Prepare to yield to oncoming traffic

C. ▢ Proceed without stopping

D. ▢ Stop and wait for a green signal

**12. What should you do if your vehicle's brakes fail?**

A. ▢ Slam on the brakes repeatedly

B. ▢ Shift into a lower gear

C. ▢ Engage the parking brake

D. ▢ Pump the brakes rapidly

**13. What is the primary purpose of wearing a seat belt?**

A. ▢ To keep you comfortable while driving

B. ▢ To enhance your vehicle's safety features

C. ▢ To prevent you from being ejected in a crash

D. ▢ To avoid getting a traffic citation

**14.What should you do if your vehicle starts to hydroplane on wet roads?**

A. ▢ Slam on the brakes

B. ▢ Accelerate to regain control

C. ▢ Steer sharply in the opposite direction

D. ▢ Gradually release the accelerator and steer straight

**15. What is the purpose of the catalytic converter in a vehicle's exhaust system?**

A. ▢ To increase fuel efficiency

B. ▢ To enhance engine performance

C. ▢ To reduce harmful emissions

D. ▢ To control vehicle noise

# Correct answers for vehicle control and safety exam 3

1. **B**. Treat it as a stop sign

2. **B**. When driving in heavy rain or snow

3. **B**. Shift into neutral

4. **C**. Proceed with caution

5. **B**. Only during foggy or misty weather conditions

6. **B**. To provide a wider field of vision

7. **B**. Keep your low beams on and look to the right side of the road

8. **C**. To provide a smooth and comfortable ride

9. **A**. Treat it as a stop sign and proceed with caution

10. **B**. Shift into neutral

11. **B**. Prepare to yield to oncoming traffic

12. **D**. Pump the brakes rapidly

13. **C**. To prevent you from being ejected in a crash

14. **D**. Gradually release the accelerator and steer straight

15. **C**. To reduce harmful emissions

# Vehicle control and safety exam 4

**1. What should you do if you notice that your vehicle's steering wheel is vibrating while driving?**

A. ▢ Ignore it and continue driving

B. ▢ Increase your driving speed to smooth out the vibrations

C. ▢ Reduce your driving speed and have the vehicle inspected

D. ▢ Turn the steering wheel in the opposite direction to correct the vibration

**2. When should you use your headlights while driving?**

A. ▢ Only during daylight hours

B. ▢ During rain or foggy weather conditions

C. ▢ When driving on well-lit city streets

D. ▢ When following another vehicle closely

**3. What should you do if your vehicle's tire blows out while driving?**

A. ▢ Slam on the brakes immediately

B. ▢ Accelerate to maintain control of the vehicle

C. ▢ Steer in the opposite direction of the blowout

D. ▢ Gradually release the accelerator and maintain a firm grip on the steering wheel

**4. What does it mean if your vehicle's check engine light is illuminated?**

A. ▢ Your vehicle is running low on fuel

B. ▢ Your vehicle's air conditioning system is malfunctioning

C. ▢ There is a problem with your vehicle's engine

D. ▢ You need to change your vehicle's oil

**5. When should you use your high beams while driving?**

A. ▢ In well-lit urban areas

B. ▢ Only during daylight hours

C. ▢ When other vehicles are approaching from the opposite direction

D. ▢ When driving on unlit rural roads

**6. What is the purpose of the rearview mirror in your vehicle?**

A. ▢ To enhance the vehicle's aesthetics

B. ▢ To provide a wider field of vision

C. ▢ To eliminate blind spots completely

D. ▢ To reflect the driver's face for identification purposes

**7. What should you do if you encounter a vehicle with its hazard lights on?**

A. ▢ Flash your high beams at the vehicle

B. ▢ Maintain your current driving speed and position

C. ▢ Slow down and proceed with caution

D. ▢ Honk your horn to get the driver's attention

**8. What is the purpose of the vehicle's suspension system?**

A. ▢ To improve fuel efficiency

B. ▢ To enhance the vehicle's aerodynamics

C. ▢ To provide a smooth and comfortable ride

D. ▢ To reduce engine noise and vibrations

**9. What should you do if you approach an intersection with malfunctioning traffic lights?**

A. ▢ Treat it as a four-way stop and proceed with caution

B. ▢ Ignore the traffic lights and proceed through the intersection

C. ▢ Drive at increased speed to clear the intersection quickly

D. ▢ Honk your horn to alert other drivers

**10. What should you do if your vehicle's accelerator becomes stuck?**

A. ▢ Slam on the brakes repeatedly

B. ▢ Shift into neutral

C. ▢ Turn off the ignition

D. ▢ Steer into oncoming traffic

**11. What does a flashing yellow traffic signal indicate?**

A. ▢ Stop and proceed with caution

B. ▢ Prepare to yield to oncoming traffic

C. ▢ Proceed without stopping

D. ▢ Stop and wait for a green signal

**12. What should you do if your vehicle's brakes fail?**

A. ▢ Slam on the brakes repeatedly

B. ▢ Shift into a lower gear

C. ▢ Engage the parking brake

D. ▢ Pump the brakes rapidly

**13. What is the primary purpose of wearing a seat belt?**

A. ▢ To keep you comfortable while driving

B. ▢ To enhance your vehicle's safety features

C. ▢ To prevent you from being ejected in a crash

D. ▢ To avoid getting a traffic citation

**14. What should you do if you encounter a vehicle driving the wrong way on a one-way street?**

A. ▢ Drive around the vehicle and continue on your way

B. ▢ Honk your horn and proceed with caution

C. ▢ Slow down, pull over, and call the police

D. ▢ Flash your headlights to warn the driver

**15. What is the purpose of the catalytic converter in a vehicle's exhaust system?**

A. ▢ To increase fuel efficiency

B. ▢ To enhance engine performance

C. ▢ To reduce harmful emissions

D. ▢ To control vehicle noise

# Correct answers for vehicle control and safety exam 4

1. **C.** Reduce your driving speed and have the vehicle inspected

2. **B.** During rain or foggy weather conditions

3. **D**. Gradually release the accelerator and maintain a firm grip on the steering wheel

4. **C.** There is a problem with your vehicle's engine

5. **D**. When driving on unlit rural roads

6. **B**. To provide a wider field of vision

7. **C**. Slow down and proceed with caution

8. **C**. To provide a smooth and comfortable ride

9. **A**. Treat it as a four-way stop and proceed with caution

10. **B**. Shift into neutral

11. **B**. Prepare to yield to oncoming traffic

12. **D**. Pump the brakes rapidly

13. **C**. To prevent you from being ejected in a crash

14. **C**. Slow down, pull over, and call the police

15. **C**. To reduce harmful emissions

# Vehicle control and safety exam 5

**1. How often should you check your vehicle's tire pressure?**

A. ▢ Once a year

B. ▢ Every six months

C. ▢ Before every long trip

D. ▢ Only when the tires look visibly deflated

**2. What is the purpose of the anti-lock braking system (ABS) in a vehicle?**

A. ▢ To reduce fuel consumption

B. ▢ To prevent tire blowouts

C. ▢ To improve vehicle stability during braking

D. ▢ To eliminate the need for regular brake maintenance

**3. What should you do if your vehicle starts to skid while driving on a slippery surface?**

A. ▢ Brake hard to regain control

B. ▢ Turn the steering wheel in the opposite direction of the skid

C. ▢ Accelerate to gain traction

D. ▢ Steer in the direction you want to go

**4. What is the purpose of the blind spot mirror or convex mirror on the side of your vehicle?**

A. ▢ To display rearview camera footage

B. ▢ To eliminate blind spots completely

C. ▢ To provide a wider field of view

D. ▢ To enhance the vehicle's aesthetics

**5. What should you do if your vehicle's accelerator becomes stuck while driving?**

A. ▢ Slam on the brakes repeatedly

B. ▢ Shift into neutral

C. ▢ Turn off the ignition

D. ▢ Steer into oncoming traffic

**6. How far in advance should you signal your intention to turn or change lanes?**

A. ▢ At least 100 feet

B. ▢ Only when other vehicles are nearby

C. ▢ Immediately before making the maneuver

D. ▢ Signal? I don't need to signal!

**7. What should you do if you experience a sudden tire blowout while driving?**

A. ▢ Swerve to the side of the road

B. ▢ Slam on the brakes immediately

C. ▢ Gradually release the accelerator and maintain a firm grip on the steering wheel

D. ▢ Speed up to get to the nearest service station

**8. How often should you check your vehicle's engine oil level?**

A. ▢ Every month

B. ▢ Once a year

C. ▢ Before every long trip

D. ▢ Only when the oil warning light illuminates

**9. What should you do if you encounter a bicyclist on the road?**

A. ▢ Honk your horn to alert them

B. ▢ Maintain your current speed and position

C. ▢ Slow down and give them ample space

D. ▢ Overtake them as quickly as possible

**10. What should you do if your vehicle's headlights suddenly fail while driving at night?**

A. ▢ Continue driving using the high beams

B. ▢ Turn on the hazard lights and drive slowly

C. ▢ Pull over to the side of the road immediately

D. ▢ Drive close to the vehicle in front to use its headlights

**11. When should you use your vehicle's hazard lights?**

A. ▢ When you are driving in heavy traffic

B. ▢ When you are running late for an appointment

C. ▢ When your vehicle has broken down or is stopped on the side of the road

D. ▢ When you want to alert other drivers of your presence

**12. What is the purpose of the Vehicle Identification Number (VIN) on a vehicle?**

A. ▢ To track the vehicle's fuel consumption

B. ▢ To identify the vehicle's color and model

C. ▢ To determine the vehicle's weight capacity

D. ▢ To uniquely identify the vehicle for registration and identification purposes

**13. What should you do if you suspect your vehicle's brakes are not functioning properly?**

A. ▢ Ignore it and continue driving

B. ▢ Pump the brakes vigorously to build up pressure

C. ▢ Have the brakes inspected and repaired by a qualified mechanic

D. ▢ Drive at a slower speed to compensate for the brake issue

**14. What is the purpose of the vehicle's rearview camera system?**

A. ▢ To provide a clear view of the vehicle's rear for reversing

B. ▢ To enhance the vehicle's aerodynamics

C. ▢ To display real-time traffic updates

D. ▢ To alert the driver of nearby vehicles or obstacles

**15. What should you do if you encounter an aggressive driver on the road?**

A. ▢ Engage in aggressive driving behavior to assert dominance

B. ▢ Ignore the driver and continue driving normally

C. ▢ Avoid eye contact and give the driver plenty of space

D. ▢ Honk your horn and make aggressive gestures to show your frustration

# Correct answers for vehicle control and safety exam 5

**1. C.** Before every long trip

**2. C.** To improve vehicle stability during braking

**3. D.** Steer in the direction you want to go

**4. C.** To provide a wider field of view

**5. B**. Shift into neutral

**6. A.** At least 100 feet

**7. C.** Gradually release the accelerator and maintain a firm grip on the steering wheel

**8. A**. Every month

**9. C.** Slow down and give them ample space

**10. C**. Pull over to the side of the road immediately

**11. C**. When your vehicle has broken down or is stopped on the side of the road

**12. D.** To uniquely identify the vehicle for registration and identification purposes

**13. C.** Have the brakes inspected and repaired by a qualified mechanic

**14. A.** To provide a clear view of the vehicle's rear for reversing

**15. C**. Avoid eye contact and give the driver plenty of space

# Alcohol and drugs

Welcome to Chapter 3 of the Minnesota DMV Exam Workbook, where we delve into the critical topic of alcohol and drugs and their impact on road safety. In this chapter, we will explore the dangers associated with driving under the influence, the legal consequences of impaired driving, and strategies to prevent and discourage this dangerous behavior. Understanding the effects of alcohol and drugs on driving abilities is crucial for creating a safer road environment in the Land of 10,000 Lakes.

## Supporting Responsible Choices

This section will explore the importance of community support and intervention to promote responsible choices regarding alcohol and drugs. We will discuss strategies such as offering alternative transportation options, encouraging designated drivers, and fostering a culture of responsible alcohol consumption. By collectively advocating for responsible choices, we can work towards reducing impaired driving incidents.

As we delve deeper into this chapter, remember that the decisions we make regarding alcohol and drugs have far-reaching consequences. By understanding the dangers, consequences, and prevention strategies associated with impaired driving, we can contribute to a safer and more responsible driving culture in Minnesota. So, let's embark on this journey towards safeguarding our roads and ensuring the well-being of all who travel upon them.

For training purposes, you can mark the ▢ symbol next to what you think is the correct answer: Once you have chosen the correct answer, use a pencil or pen to mark the ▢ symbol next to that answer.

# Alcohol and drugs exam

**1. What is the legal blood alcohol concentration (BAC) limit for most adult drivers in the United States?**

A. ▢ 0.01%

B. ▢ 0.05%

C. ▢ 0.08%

D. ▢ 0.10%

**2. Which of the following is NOT a common symptom of alcohol impairment?**

A. ▢ Slurred speech

B. ▢ Increased coordination

C. ▢ Impaired judgment

D. ▢ Slow reaction time

**3. What is the implied consent law in relation to driving under the influence (DUI) or driving while intoxicated (DWI)?**

A. ▢ It allows law enforcement to test your BAC without your consent

B. ▢ It allows you to refuse a breathalyzer test without consequences

C. ▢ It requires law enforcement to obtain a warrant to test your BAC

D. ▢ It applies only to underage drivers

**4. Which of the following drugs can impair your ability to drive safely?**

A. ▢ Over-the-counter cold medication

B. ▢ Prescription painkillers

C. ▢ Marijuana

D. ▢ All of the above

**5. What is the best way to sober up quickly after consuming alcohol?**

A. ▢ Drinking coffee

B. ▢ Taking a cold shower

C. ▢ Eating a large meal

D. ▢ Time is the only way to sober up

**6. What does the term "zero tolerance" mean in relation to driving under the influence of alcohol or drugs?**

A. ▢ It refers to the complete ban on alcohol or drugs while driving

B. ▢ It means you can have a small amount of alcohol or drugs in your system while driving

C. ▢ It applies only to drivers under the age of 21

D. ▢ It allows you to have a designated driver if you are impaired

**7. What are the potential penalties for a first-time DUI conviction?**

A. ▢ License suspension, fines, and possible jail time

B. ▢ Mandatory alcohol education program

C. ▢ Increased insurance rates

D. ▢ All of the above

**8. How does alcohol affect your driving abilities?**

A. ▢ It improves reaction time and coordination

B. ▢ It enhances your vision and depth perception

C. ▢ It impairs judgment and reduces coordination

D. ▢ It has no effect on driving abilities

**9. What should you do if you suspect another driver is under the influence of alcohol or drugs?**

A. ▢ Ignore it and continue driving

B. ▢ Tailgate them to force them to pull over

C. ▢ Maintain a safe distance and contact law enforcement

D. ▢ Flash your headlights to alert them

**10. How can prescription medications affect your driving abilities?**

A. ▢ They have no effect on driving abilities

B. ▢ They can cause drowsiness or impair judgment

C. ▢ They improve reaction time and coordination

D. ▢ They enhance vision and depth perception

**11. What does the term "drugged driving" refer to?**

A. ▢ Driving under the influence of illegal drugs only

B. ▢ Driving under the influence of prescription drugs only

C. ▢ Driving under the influence of any impairing substance, including drugs

D. ▢ Driving while feeling tired or fatigued

**12. What is the purpose of a roadside sobriety test?**

A. ▢ To determine the type of alcohol consumed

B. ▢ To estimate the driver's blood alcohol concentration (BAC)

C. ▢ To assess the driver's physical fitness level

D. ▢ To measure the driver's reaction time

**13. What is the legal drinking age in most states in the United States?**

A. ▢ 18 years old

B. ▢ 19 years old

C. ▢ 21 years old

D. ▢ 25 years old

**14. What is the best way to avoid driving under the influence of alcohol or drugs?**

A. ▢ Designate a sober driver or use public transportation

B. ▢ Drink alcohol in moderation

C. ▢ Understand the effects of prescription medications

D. ▢ All of the above

**15. How long does it take for the effects of alcohol to wear off?**

A. ▢ 1 hour

B. ▢ 3 hours

C. ▢ 6 hours

D. ▢ It varies depending on the individual and the amount consumed

# Correct answers for alcohol and drugs exam

1. **C**. 0.08%

2. **B**. Increased coordination

3. **A.** It allows law enforcement to test your BAC without your consent

4. **D**. All of the above

5. **D.** Time is the only way to sober up

6. **C.** It applies only to drivers under the age of 21

7. **D.** All of the above

8. **C.** It impairs judgment and reduces coordination

9. **C.** Maintain a safe distance and contact law enforcement

10. **B.** They can cause drowsiness or impair judgment

11. **C.** Driving under the influence of any impairing substance, including drugs

12. **B.** To estimate the driver's blood alcohol concentration (BAC)

13. **C.** 21 years old

14. **D.** All of the above

15. **D.** It varies depending on the individual and the amount consumed

# Alcohol and drugs exam 2

**1. What is the legal limit for marijuana impairment while driving in most states?**

A. ▢ 0.01%

B. ▢ 0.05%

C. ▢ 0.08%

D. ▢ There is no set limit

**2. Which of the following is an effect of alcohol on driving performance?**

A. ▢ Improved concentration

B. ▢ Increased alertness

C. ▢ Reduced reaction time

D. ▢ Enhanced vision

**3. What is the purpose of field sobriety tests during a traffic stop?**

A. ▢ To measure the driver's blood alcohol concentration (BAC)

B. ▢ To assess the driver's physical fitness level

C. ▢ To determine the type of alcohol consumed

D. ▢ To evaluate the driver's coordination and impairment

**4. Which of the following factors can affect the rate at which alcohol affects an individual?**

A. ▢ Gender

B. ▢ Body weight

C. ▢ Type of alcohol consumed

D. ▢ All of the above

**5. How does alcohol impact a driver's ability to judge distances?**

A. ▢ It improves depth perception

B. ▢ It enhances peripheral vision

C. ▢ It impairs depth perception

D. ▢ It has no effect on judging distances

**6. What is the purpose of a breathalyzer test?**

A. ▢ To measure the level of alcohol in a driver's system

B. ▢ To determine the driver's blood type

C. ▢ To assess the driver's coordination and balance

D. ▢ To test the driver's vision

**7. Which of the following medications can impair your ability to drive safely?**

A. ▢ Antihistamines

B. ▢ Antidepressants

C. ▢ Painkillers

D. ▢ All of the above

**8. What is the legal consequence for refusing a breathalyzer test when suspected of DUI?**

A. ▢ A fine

B. ▢ License suspension

C. ▢ Jail time

D. ▢ All of the above

**9. How does alcohol affect a driver's judgment and decision-making abilities?**

A. ▢ It improves judgment and decision-making

B. ▢ It enhances risk assessment skills

C. ▢ It impairs judgment and decision-making

D. ▢ It has no effect on judgment and decision-making

**10. What is the purpose of an ignition interlock device?**

A. ▢ To test the driver's reaction time

B. ▢ To measure the driver's blood alcohol concentration (BAC)

C. ▢ To lock the vehicle's ignition if alcohol is detected

D. ▢ To monitor the vehicle's speed and location

**11. How does marijuana use impact a driver's ability to operate a vehicle safely?**

A. ▢ It improves coordination and reaction time

B. ▢ It enhances vision and perception

C. ▢ It impairs judgment, coordination, and reaction time

D. ▢ It has no effect on driving abilities

**12. What is the legal consequence for driving under the influence of drugs?**

A. ▢ A warning

B. ▢ A small fine

C. ▢ License suspension, fines, and possible jail time

D. ▢ Mandatory drug education program

**13. How does alcohol affect a driver's concentration and attention span?**

A. ▢ It improves concentration and attention span

B. ▢ It enhances focus and multitasking abilities

C. ▢ It impairs concentration and attention span

D. ▢ It has no effect on concentration and attention span

**14. What is the best way to prevent drug-impaired driving?**

A. ▢ Avoid taking any medications

B. ▢ Understand the side effects of prescribed medications

C. ▢ Seek alternative transportation if impaired

D. ▢ All of the above

**15. How does alcohol impact a driver's reaction time?**

A. ▢ It improves reaction time

B. ▢ It has no effect on reaction time

C. ▢ It slows down reaction time

D. ▢ It enhances reflexes

## Correct answers for alcohol and drugs exam 2

1. **D.** There is no set limit

2. **C.** Reduced reaction time

3. **D.** To evaluate the driver's coordination and impairment

4. **D**. All of the above

5. **C**. It impairs depth perception

6. **A**. To measure the level of alcohol in a driver's system

7. **D**. All of the above

8. **D.** All of the above

9. **C.** It impairs judgment and decision-making

10. **C.** To lock the vehicle's ignition if alcohol is detected

11. **C.** It impairs judgment, coordination, and reaction time

12. **C.** License suspension, fines, and possible jail time

13. **C.** It impairs concentration and attention span

14. **D.** All of the above

15. **C.** It slows down reaction time

# Alcohol and drugs exam 3

**1. What is the legal blood alcohol concentration (BAC) limit for commercial vehicle drivers in most states?**

A. ▢ 0.04%

B. ▢ 0.08%

C. ▢ 0.10%

D. ▢ 0.12%

**2. How does alcohol consumption affect a driver's ability to track moving objects?**

A. ▢ It improves tracking abilities

B. ▢ It enhances peripheral vision

C. ▢ It impairs tracking abilities

D. ▢ It has no effect on tracking abilities

**3. What is the purpose of implied consent laws regarding chemical tests?**

A. ▢ To determine the type of drugs consumed

B. ▢ To assess the driver's physical fitness level

C. ▢ To estimate the driver's blood alcohol concentration (BAC)

D. ▢ To evaluate the driver's coordination and impairment

**4. Which of the following factors can influence how alcohol affects an individual?**

A. ▢ Body size and composition

B. ▢ Tolerance to alcohol

C. ▢ The presence of other drugs in the system

D. ▢ All of the above

**5. How does alcohol affect a driver's ability to judge speed?**

A. ▢ It improves speed perception

B. ▢ It enhances reaction time

C. ▢ It impairs speed perception

D. ▢ It has no effect on judging speed

**6. What is the purpose of a blood test during a DUI stop?**

A. ▢ To measure the driver's blood alcohol concentration (BAC)

B. ▢ To determine the driver's blood type

C. ▢ To assess the driver's coordination and balance

D. ▢ To test the driver's vision

**7. Which of the following medications can impair a driver's ability to operate a vehicle safely?**

A. ▢ Antipsychotics

B. ▢ Muscle relaxants

C. ▢ Sleep aids

D. ▢ All of the above

**8. What is the penalty for a first-time DUI offense?**

A. ▢ A warning

B. ▢ A small fine

C. ▢ License suspension, fines, and possible jail time

D. ▢ Mandatory participation in a rehabilitation program

**9. How does alcohol impact a driver's perception of risks and consequences?**

A. ▢ It improves risk assessment skills

B. ▢ It enhances decision-making abilities

C. ▢ It impairs risk perception and judgment

D. ▢ It has no effect on risk perception

**10. What is the purpose of drug recognition experts (DREs) in DUI cases?**

A. ▢ To administer field sobriety tests

B. ▢ To determine the driver's blood alcohol concentration (BAC)

C. ▢ To assess the driver's physical fitness level

D. ▢ To evaluate drug impairment in drivers

**11. How does marijuana use impact a driver's coordination and motor skills?**

A. ▢ It improves coordination and motor skills

B. ▢ It enhances reaction time

C. ▢ It impairs coordination and motor skills

D. ▢ It has no effect on coordination and motor skills

**12. What is the legal consequence for driving under the influence of drugs?**

A. ▢ A small fine

B. ▢ A warning

C. ▢ License suspension, fines, and possible jail time

D. ▢ Mandatory community service

**13. How does alcohol affect a driver's ability to maintain lane position?**

A. ▢ It improves lane positioning

B. ▢ It enhances steering control

C. ▢ It impairs lane positioning

D. ▢ It has no effect on maintaining lane position

**14. What is the purpose of an ignition interlock device (IID)?**

A. ▢ To measure the driver's reaction time

B. ▢ To determine the driver's blood alcohol concentration (BAC)

C. ▢ To lock the vehicle's ignition if alcohol is detected

D. ▢ To monitor the vehicle's speed and location

**15. How does alcohol impact a driver's decision-making abilities?**

A. ▢ It improves decision-making skills

B. ▢ It enhances judgment in risky situations

C. ▢ It impairs decision-making abilities

D. ▢ It has no effect on decision-making

# Correct answers for alcohol and drugs exam 3

1. **A**. 0.04%

2. **C**. It impairs tracking abilities

3. **C**. To estimate the driver's blood alcohol concentration (BAC)

4. **D**. All of the above

5. **C**. It impairs speed perception

6. **A**. To measure the driver's blood alcohol concentration (BAC)

7. **D**. All of the above

8. **C**. License suspension, fines, and possible jail time

9. **C**. It impairs risk perception and judgment

10. **D**. To evaluate drug impairment in drivers

11. **C**. It impairs coordination and motor skills

12. **C**. License suspension, fines, and possible jail time

13. **C**. It impairs lane positioning

14. **C**. To lock the vehicle's ignition if alcohol is detected

15. **C**. It impairs decision-making abilities

# Alcohol and drugs exam 4

**1. What is the legal blood alcohol concentration (BAC) limit for drivers under the age of 21 in most states?**

A. ▢ 0.02%

B. ▢ 0.04%

C. ▢ 0.06%

D. ▢ 0.08%

**2. How does alcohol consumption affect a driver's vision?**

A. ▢ It improves night vision

B. ▢ It enhances peripheral vision

C. ▢ It impairs vision, particularly depth perception and peripheral vision

D. ▢ It has no effect on vision

**3. What is the purpose of field sobriety tests during a DUI stop?**

A. ▢ To measure the driver's blood alcohol concentration (BAC)

B. ▢ To determine the driver's blood type

C. ▢ To assess the driver's coordination and impairment

D. ▢ To test the driver's reaction time

**4. Which of the following drugs can impair a driver's ability to operate a vehicle safely?**

A. ▢ Opioids

B. ▢ Stimulants

C. ▢ Sedatives

D. ▢ All of the above

**5. How does alcohol affect a driver's ability to judge distances?**

A. ▢ It improves distance estimation

B. ▢ It enhances reaction time

C. ▢ It impairs distance judgment

D. ▢ It has no effect on judging distances

**6. What is the purpose of a breathalyzer test during a DUI stop?**

A. ▢ To measure the driver's blood alcohol concentration (BAC)

B. ▢ To determine the driver's lung capacity

C. ▢ To assess the driver's coordination and balance

D. ▢ To test the driver's hearing acuity

**7. Which of the following factors can influence how drugs affect an individual's driving abilities?**

A. ▢ Dosage and potency

B. ▢ Tolerance to the drug

C. ▢ The presence of other drugs in the system

D. ▢ All of the above

**8. What is the penalty for refusing a chemical test during a DUI stop?**

A. ▢ A warning

B. ▢ A small fine

C. ▢ License suspension, fines, and possible jail time

D. ▢ Mandatory participation in a rehabilitation program

**9. How does alcohol impact a driver's ability to make safe and timely decisions?**

A. ▢ It improves decision-making abilities

B. ▢ It enhances risk assessment skills

C. ▢ It impairs judgment and decision-making abilities

D. ▢ It has no effect on decision-making

**10. What is the purpose of the Drug Evaluation and Classification Program (DECP)?**

A. ▢ To administer field sobriety tests

B. ▢ To determine the driver's blood alcohol concentration (BAC)

C. ▢ To assess the driver's physical fitness level

D. ▢ To evaluate drug impairment in drivers

**11. How does marijuana use impact a driver's attention and focus?**

A. ▢ It improves attention and focus

B. ▢ It enhances reaction time

C. ▢ It impairs attention and focus

D. ▢ It has no effect on attention and focus

**12. What is the legal consequence for a repeat DUI offense?**

A. ▢ A small fine

B. ▢ A warning

C. ▢ License suspension, fines, and possible jail time

D. ▢ Mandatory participation in a drug education program

**13. How does alcohol affect a driver's ability to react to sudden hazards?**

A. ▢ It improves reaction time

B. ▢ It enhances peripheral vision

C. ▢ It impairs reaction time

D. ▢ It has no effect on reaction time

**14. What is the purpose of a urine test during a DUI stop?**

A. ▢ To measure the driver's blood alcohol concentration (BAC)

B. ▢ To determine the driver's urine acidity level

C. ▢ To assess the driver's coordination and balance

D. ▢ To test the driver's kidney function

**15. How does alcohol impact a driver's coordination and motor skills?**

A. ▢ It improves coordination and motor skills

B. ▢ It enhances reaction time

C. ▢ It impairs coordination and motor skills

D. ▢ It has no effect on coordination and motor skills

# Correct answers for alcohol and drugs exam 4

**1. A.** 0.02%

**2. C.** It impairs vision, particularly depth perception and peripheral vision

**3. C.** To assess the driver's coordination and impairment

**4. D.** All of the above

**5. C.** It impairs distance judgment

**6. A.** To measure the driver's blood alcohol concentration (BAC)

**7. D.** All of the above

**8. C.** License suspension, fines, and possible jail time

**9. C.** It impairs judgment and decision-making abilities

**10. D.** To evaluate drug impairment in drivers

**11. C.** It impairs attention and focus

**12. C.** License suspension, fines, and possible jail time

**13. C.** It impairs reaction time

**14. A.** To measure the driver's blood alcohol concentration (BAC)

**15. C.** It impairs coordination and motor skills

# Alcohol and drugs exam 5

**1. What is the legal blood alcohol concentration (BAC) limit for commercial drivers in most states?**

A. ▢ 0.02%

B. ▢ 0.04%

C. ▢ 0.06%

D. ▢ 0.08%

**2. How does alcohol consumption affect a driver's coordination and motor skills?**

A. ▢ It improves coordination and motor skills

B. ▢ It enhances reaction time

C. ▢ It impairs coordination and motor skills

D. ▢ It has no effect on coordination and motor skills

**3. What is the purpose of the Advanced Roadside Impaired Driving Enforcement (ARIDE) program?**

A. ▢ To administer field sobriety tests

B. ▢ To determine the driver's blood alcohol concentration (BAC)

C. ▢ To assess the driver's physical fitness level

D. ▢ To train officers to recognize drug-impaired driving

**4. Which of the following drugs can impair a driver's ability to concentrate?**

A. ▢ Marijuana

B. ▢ Antihistamines

C. ▢ Performance-enhancing drugs

D. ▢ All of the above

**5. How does alcohol affect a driver's ability to perceive and respond to traffic signals?**

A. ▢ It improves signal recognition

B. ▢ It enhances reaction time

C. ▢ It impairs signal recognition and response

D. ▢ It has no effect on signal perception

**6. What is the purpose of a blood test during a DUI stop?**

A. ▢ To measure the driver's blood alcohol concentration (BAC)

B. ▢ To determine the driver's blood type

C. ▢ To assess the driver's coordination and balance

D. ▢ To test the driver's blood sugar levels

**7. Which of the following factors can affect how drugs impact an individual's driving abilities?**

A. ▢ Body weight and metabolism

B. ▢ The presence of other drugs or medications

C. ▢ The frequency and amount of drug use

D. ▢ All of the above

**8. What is the penalty for driving under the influence of drugs or alcohol for a second offense?**

A. ▢ A warning

B. ▢ A small fine

C. ▢ License suspension, fines, and possible jail time

D. ▢ Mandatory participation in a rehabilitation program

**9. How does alcohol impact a driver's ability to perceive and respond to potential hazards?**

A. ▢ It improves hazard recognition

B. ▢ It enhances peripheral vision

C. ▢ It impairs hazard perception and response

D. ▢ It has no effect on hazard perception

**10. What is the purpose of the Drug Recognition Expert (DRE) evaluation during a DUI stop?**

A. ▢ To administer field sobriety tests

B. ▢ To determine the driver's blood alcohol concentration (BAC)

C. ▢ To assess the driver's physical fitness level

D. ▢ To determine the presence of drug impairment

**11. How does the use of hallucinogenic drugs affect a driver's ability to make sound judgments?**

A. ▢ It improves judgment and decision-making abilities

B. ▢ It enhances risk assessment skills

C. ▢ It impairs judgment and decision-making abilities

D. ▢ It has no effect on judgment and decision-making

**12. What is the legal consequence for refusing a chemical test during a DUI stop?**

A. ▢ A written warning

B. ▢ A small fine

C. ▢ License suspension, fines, and possible jail time

D. ▢ Completion of a defensive driving course

**13. How does alcohol affect a driver's ability to maintain a steady speed?**

A. ▢ It improves speed control

B. ▢ It enhances reaction time

C. ▢ It impairs speed control

D. ▢ It has no effect on speed control

**14. What is the purpose of the Drug Evaluation and Classification Program (DECP)?**

A. ▢ To determine the driver's blood alcohol concentration (BAC)

B. ▢ To assess the driver's physical fitness level

C. ▢ To evaluate drug impairment in drivers

D. ▢ To provide rehabilitation programs for drug users

**15. How does cocaine use impact a driver's attention and focus?**

A. ▢ It improves attention and focus

B. ▢ It enhances reaction time

C. ▢ It impairs attention and focus

D. ▢ It has no effect on attention and focus

# Correct answers for alcohol and drugs exam 5

**1. D.** 0.08%

**2. C.** It impairs coordination and motor skills

**3. D.** To train officers to recognize drug-impaired driving

**4. D**. All of the above

**5. C.** It impairs signal recognition and response

**6. A.** To measure the driver's blood alcohol concentration (BAC)

**7. D.** All of the above

**8. C**. License suspension, fines, and possible jail time

**9. C.** It impairs hazard perception and response

**10. D.** To determine the presence of drug impairment

**11. C.** It impairs judgment and decision-making abilities

**12. C.** License suspension, fines, and possible jail time

**13. C**. It impairs speed control

**14. C**. To evaluate drug impairment in drivers

**15. C**. It impairs attention and focus

# Vehicle equipment and maintenance

Welcome to Chapter 4 of the Minnesota DMV Exam Workbook, where we explore the critical aspects of vehicle equipment and maintenance. In this chapter, we will delve into the essential components and systems that contribute to a vehicle's roadworthiness and the importance of regular maintenance. Understanding vehicle equipment requirements and implementing proper maintenance practices are key factors in promoting safety, reliability, and efficiency on Minnesota's roads.

-Vehicle equipment and maintenance are integral parts of responsible vehicle ownership and safe driving. This section will emphasize the significance of maintaining a properly equipped and well-maintained vehicle. We will discuss the direct correlation between vehicle condition and road safety, highlighting the importance of regular inspections and maintenance to ensure optimal performance.

## Minnesota Vehicle Equipment Requirements

Minnesota has specific requirements regarding vehicle equipment to ensure safety and compliance with state laws. This section will provide an overview of the equipment requirements, including lighting and signaling devices, mirrors, tires, brakes, windshield wipers, and exhaust systems. Understanding and adhering to these requirements are crucial for both legal compliance and the safety of yourself and others on the road.

## Lighting and Signaling Devices

Proper lighting and signaling devices are essential for visibility and communication on the road. This section will delve into the different lighting and signaling devices required in Minnesota, including headlights, taillights, turn signals, brake lights, and reflectors. We will discuss their functions, proper usage, and maintenance. Understanding how to effectively utilize these devices enhances visibility and ensures that your intentions are communicated to other drivers.

## Tire Maintenance and Safety

Tires play a critical role in vehicle safety and performance. This section will focus on tire maintenance and safety practices, including checking tire pressure, inspecting tread depth, and ensuring proper alignment. We will discuss the importance of regular tire maintenance, the risks associated with worn or damaged tires, and the benefits of using appropriate tires for different weather conditions.

## Braking Systems

Brakes are the primary safety feature of any vehicle, and maintaining their effectiveness is crucial for safe driving. This section will cover the different types of braking systems, such as disc brakes and drum brakes, and the importance of regular brake inspections and maintenance. We will also discuss common signs of brake wear and the importance of addressing brake-related issues promptly to ensure optimal braking performance.

## Windshield and Wiper Maintenance

Clear visibility is essential for safe driving. This section will explore the importance of windshield and wiper maintenance. We will discuss the significance of keeping the windshield clean, inspecting for cracks or chips, and replacing worn wiper blades. Additionally, we will provide tips for using windshield washer fluid effectively to maintain a clear field of vision.

## Vehicle Fluids and Lubricants

Proper fluid levels and lubrication are vital for the smooth operation of a vehicle. This section will cover the essential fluids and lubricants in a vehicle, including engine oil, coolant, transmission fluid, brake fluid, and power steering fluid. We will discuss the importance of checking fluid levels regularly, understanding the recommended specifications, and the consequences of neglecting fluid maintenance.

## Exhaust Emission Control Systems

Reducing harmful emissions is an essential aspect of vehicle maintenance. This section will discuss the exhaust emission control systems in vehicles, such as catalytic converters and oxygen sensors. We will explore the purpose of these systems, their role in environmental conservation, and the importance of regular inspections to ensure compliance with emission standards.

## Routine Maintenance and Inspections

Regular maintenance and inspections are critical for keeping a vehicle in optimal condition. This section will provide a comprehensive overview of routine maintenance tasks, including oil changes, filter replacements, belt inspections, battery maintenance, and tire rotations. We will emphasize the importance of following the manufacturer's recommended maintenance schedule and keeping accurate maintenance records.

## Vehicle Safety Checks

Performing regular safety checks is an integral part of vehicle maintenance. This section will outline safety checks that should be conducted before each trip, such as checking seat belts, adjusting mirrors, testing horn functionality, and inspecting emergency equipment. By incorporating safety checks into your pre-drive routine, you can identify potential issues and ensure a safe driving experience

By understanding the importance of vehicle equipment and maintenance, you are taking proactive steps towards safer, more efficient driving in Minnesota.

For training purposes, you can mark the ▢ symbol next to what you think is the correct answer: Once you have chosen the correct answer, use a pencil or pen to mark the ▢ symbol next to that answer.

# Vehicle equipment and maintenance exam

**1. What should you do if your vehicle's tire pressure is lower than recommended?**

A. ▢ Inflate the tire to the recommended pressure

B. ▢ Continue driving without adjusting the tire pressure

C. ▢ Overinflate the tire for better performance

D. ▢ Reduce the vehicle's weight to compensate for low tire pressure

**2. When should you replace your vehicle's windshield wipers?**

A. ▢ Every month

B. ▢ Every year

C. ▢ When they show signs of wear or damage

D. ▢ Only if they are not working during rain

**3. What should you do if your vehicle's headlights are not working properly?**

A. ▢ Use high beams instead

B. ▢ Drive with the hazard lights on

C. ▢ Replace the bulbs or get them repaired

D. ▢ Ignore the issue if it's only a minor problem

**4. What is the purpose of the vehicle's catalytic converter?**

A. ▢ To increase fuel efficiency

B. ▢ To reduce emissions

C. ▢ To improve engine performance

D. ▢ To regulate tire pressure

**5. How often should you check the engine oil level in your vehicle?**

A. ▢ Every 500 miles

B. ▢ Every month

C. ▢ Before long trips

D. ▢ Only if there is an oil leak

**6. What should you do if your vehicle's brake pedal feels spongy or goes all the way to the floor?**

A. ▢ Continue driving cautiously

B. ▢ Pump the brakes to restore pressure

C. ▢ Replace the brake pads immediately

D. ▢ Have the brakes inspected and repaired

**7. When should you replace your vehicle's air filter?**

A. ▢ Every 5,000 miles

B. ▢ Every 10,000 miles

C. ▢ Every year

D. ▢ When it appears dirty or clogged

**8. What is the purpose of the vehicle's alternator?**

A. ▢ To charge the battery

B. ▢ To regulate engine temperature

C. ▢ To control the fuel injection system

D. ▢ To improve tire traction

**9. What should you do if your vehicle's temperature gauge shows the engine is overheating?**

A. ▢ Add more coolant while the engine is running

B. ▢ Turn off the engine and wait for it to cool down

C. ▢ Continue driving at a slower speed to cool the engine

D. ▢ Ignore the gauge as it might be faulty

**10. How often should you rotate your vehicle's tires for even wear?**

A. ▢ Every 5,000 miles

B. ▢ Every 10,000 miles

C. ▢ Every 15,000 miles

D. ▢ Only if the tires show signs of uneven wear

**11. What should you do if your vehicle's check engine light is illuminated?**

A. ▢ Schedule a routine maintenance appointment

B. ▢ Ignore it unless there is a noticeable issue with the vehicle

C. ▢ Have the vehicle's diagnostic system checked

D. ▢ Reset the light using the dashboard controls

**12. When should you replace your vehicle's cabin air filter?**

A. ▢ Every 5,000 miles

B. ▢ Every 10,000 miles

C. ▢ Every year

D. ▢ Only if you notice a bad odor inside the vehicle

**13. What is the purpose of the vehicle's power steering fluid?**

A. ▢ To clean the engine's internal components

B. ▢ To provide lubrication to the transmission

C. ▢ To help with steering and maneuverability

D. ▢ To improve fuel efficiency

**14. How often should you replace your vehicle's spark plugs?**

A. ▢ Every 10,000 miles

B. ▢ Every 30,000 miles

C. ▢ Every 50,000 miles

D. ▢ Only if you experience engine misfires

**15. What should you do if your vehicle's battery is corroded?**

A. ▢ Clean the corrosion with a mixture of water and baking soda

B. ▢ Replace the battery immediately

C. ▢ Ignore the corrosion as it does not affect the battery's performance

D. ▢ Pour gasoline on the battery to dissolve the corrosion

# Correct answers for vehicle equipment and maintenance exam

1. **A.** Inflate the tire to the recommended pressure

2. **C.** When they show signs of wear or damage

3. **C.** Replace the bulbs or get them repaired

4. **B**. To reduce emissions

5. **C.** Before long trips

6. **D.** Have the brakes inspected and repaired

7. **D.** When it appears dirty or clogged

8. **A.** To charge the battery

9. **B.** Turn off the engine and wait for it to cool down

10. **A.** Every 5,000 miles

11. **C.** Have the vehicle's diagnostic system checked

12. **C**. Every year

13. **C**. To help with steering and maneuverability

14. **C.** Every 50,000 miles

15. **A.** Clean the corrosion with a mixture of water and baking soda

# Vehicle equipment and maintenance exam 2

**1. What should you do if your vehicle's tire pressure is lower than recommended?**

A. ▢ Inflate the tire to the recommended pressure

B. ▢ Continue driving without adjusting the tire pressure

C. ▢ Overinflate the tire for better performance

D. ▢ Reduce the vehicle's weight to compensate for low tire pressure

**2. When should you replace your vehicle's windshield wipers?**

A. ▢ Every month

B. ▢ Every year

C. ▢ When they show signs of wear or damage

D. ▢ Only if they are not working during rain

**3. What should you do if your vehicle's headlights are not working properly?**

A. ▢ Use high beams instead

B. ▢ Drive with the hazard lights on

C. ▢ Replace the bulbs or get them repaired

D. ▢ Ignore the issue if it's only a minor problem

**4. What is the purpose of the vehicle's catalytic converter?**

A. ▢ To increase fuel efficiency

B. ▢ To reduce emissions

C. ▢ To improve engine performance

D. ▢ To regulate tire pressure

**5. How often should you check the engine oil level in your vehicle?**

A. ▢ Every 500 miles

B. ▢ Every month

C. ▢ Before long trips

D. ▢ Only if there is an oil leak

**6. What should you do if your vehicle's brake pedal feels spongy or goes all the way to the floor?**

A. ▢ Continue driving cautiously

B. ▢ Pump the brakes to restore pressure

C. ▢ Replace the brake pads immediately

D. ▢ Have the brakes inspected and repaired

**7. When should you replace your vehicle's air filter?**

A. ▢ Every 5,000 miles

B. ▢ Every 10,000 miles

C. ▢ Every year

D. ▢ When it appears dirty or clogged

**8. What is the purpose of the vehicle's alternator?**

A. ▢ To charge the battery

B. ▢ To regulate engine temperature

C. ▢ To control the fuel injection system

D. ▢ To improve tire traction

**9. What should you do if your vehicle's temperature gauge shows the engine is overheating?**

A. ▢ Add more coolant while the engine is running

B. ▢ Turn off the engine and wait for it to cool down

C. ▢ Continue driving at a slower speed to cool the engine

D. ▢ Ignore the gauge as it might be faulty

**10. How often should you rotate your vehicle's tires for even wear?**

A. ▢ Every 5,000 miles

B. ▢ Every 10,000 miles

C. ▢ Every 15,000 miles

D. ▢ Only if the tires show signs of uneven wear

**11. What should you do if your vehicle's check engine light is illuminated?**

A. ▢ Schedule a routine maintenance appointment

B. ▢ Ignore it unless there is a noticeable issue with the vehicle

C. ▢ Have the vehicle's diagnostic system checked

D. ▢ Reset the light using the dashboard controls

**12. When should you replace your vehicle's cabin air filter?**

A. ▢ Every 5,000 miles

B. ▢ Every 10,000 miles

C. ▢ Every year

D. ▢ Only if you notice a bad odor inside the vehicle

**13. What is the purpose of the vehicle's power steering fluid?**

A. ▢ To clean the engine's internal components

B. ▢ To provide lubrication to the transmission

C. ▢ To help with steering and maneuverability

D. ▢ To improve fuel efficiency

**14. How often should you replace your vehicle's spark plugs?**

A. ▢ Every 10,000 miles

B. ▢ Every 30,000 miles

C. ▢ Every 50,000 miles

D. ▢ Only if you experience engine misfires

**15. What should you do if your vehicle's battery is corroded?**

A. ▢ Clean the corrosion with a mixture of water and baking soda

B. ▢ Replace the battery immediately

C. ▢ Ignore the corrosion as it does not affect the battery's performance

D. ▢ Pour gasoline on the battery to dissolve the corrosion

# Correct answers for Vehicle equipment and maintenance exam 2

**1. A.** Inflate the tire to the recommended pressure

**2. C.** When they show signs of wear or damage

**3. C.** Replace the bulbs or get them repaired

**4. B.** To reduce emissions

**5. C.** Before long trips

**6. D.** Have the brakes inspected and repaired

**7. D.** When it appears dirty or clogged

**8. A.** To charge the battery

**9. B.** Turn off the engine and wait for it to cool down

**10. A.** Every 5,000 miles

**11. C.** Have the vehicle's diagnostic system checked

**12. C.** Every year

**13. C.** To help with steering and maneuverability

**14. C.** Every 50,000 miles

**15. A.** Clean the corrosion with a mixture of water and baking soda

# Vehicle equipment and maintenance exam 3

**1. What is the purpose of the vehicle's alternator?**

A. ○ To charge the battery

B. ○ To control the transmission

C. ○ To regulate tire pressure

D. ○ To cool the engine

**2. How often should you check your vehicle's tire pressure?**

A. ○ Every month

B. ○ Every 6 months

C. ○ Every year

D. ○ Only if you notice a flat tire

**3. What is the purpose of the vehicle's fuel cap?**

A. ○ To prevent fuel spills

B. ○ To increase engine power

C. ○ To regulate tire pressure

D. ○ To control the transmission

**4. When should you replace your vehicle's windshield wipers?**

A. ○ Every 3 months

B. ○ Every 6 months

C. ○ Every year

D. ○ Only if they leave streaks on the windshield

**5. What is the purpose of the vehicle's catalytic converter?**

A. ▢ To enhance fuel efficiency

B. ▢ To reduce emissions

C. ▢ To control engine temperature

D. ▢ To regulate tire pressure

**6. How often should you check your vehicle's engine oil level?**

A. ▢ Every month

B. ▢ Every 3 months

C. ▢ Every 6 months

D. ▢ Only if you notice a decrease in performance

**7. What should you do if your vehicle's check engine light comes on?**

A. ▢ Ignore it as it might be a false alarm

B. ▢ Continue driving until the next service appointment

C. ▢ Have the vehicle's diagnostic system checked

D. ▢ Add more fuel to the tank

**8. What is the purpose of the vehicle's air filter?**

A. ▢ To regulate tire pressure

B. ▢ To reduce engine noise

C. ▢ To provide cleaner air to the engine

D. ▢ To control the transmission

**9. How often should you rotate your vehicle's tires?**

A. ▢ Every 5,000 miles

B. ▢ Every 10,000 miles

C. ▢ Every year

D. ▢ Only if they show signs of uneven wear


**10. What is the purpose of the vehicle's powertrain control module (PCM)?**

A. ▢ To control the transmission

B. ▢ To enhance fuel efficiency

C. ▢ To regulate tire pressure

D. ▢ To monitor and control engine performance


**11. When should you replace your vehicle's serpentine belt?**

A. ▢ Every 20,000 miles

B. ▢ Every 50,000 miles

C. ▢ Every 100,000 miles

D. ▢ Only if it shows signs of wear or damage


**12. What should you do if your vehicle's headlights appear dim?**

A. ▢ Replace the bulbs immediately

B. ▢ Clean the headlights with a mixture of soap and water

C. ▢ Have the charging system checked

D. ▢ Ignore it as it does not affect visibility

**13. How often should you check your vehicle's brake fluid level?**

A. ▢ Every month

B. ▢ Every 3 months

C. ▢ Every 6 months

D. ▢ Only if you notice a decrease in braking performance

**14. What is the purpose of the vehicle's power steering fluid?**

A. ▢ To enhance fuel efficiency

B. ▢ To control engine temperature

C. ▢ To reduce noise from the engine

D. ▢ To assist with steering and maneuverability

**15. How often should you replace your vehicle's engine air filter?**

A. ▢ Every 10,000 miles

B. ▢ Every 20,000 miles

C. ▢ Every year

D. ▢ Only if you notice a decrease in engine performance

# Correct answers for vehicle equipment and maintenance exam 3

**1. A.** To charge the battery

**2. A.** Every month

**3. A.** To prevent fuel spills

**4. B.** Every 6 months

**5. B.** To reduce emissions

**6. A.** Every month

**7. C.** Have the vehicle's diagnostic system checked

**8. C.** To provide cleaner air to the engine

**9. B.** Every 10,000 miles

**10. D.** To monitor and control engine performance

**11. D.** Only if it shows signs of wear or damage

**12. C.** Have the charging system checked

**13. A.** Every month

**14. D.** To assist with steering and maneuverability

**15. C.** Every year

# Vehicle equipment and maintenance exam 4:

**1. What is the purpose of the vehicle's radiator?**

A. ▢ To regulate tire pressure

B. ▢ To enhance fuel efficiency

C. ▢ To cool the engine

D. ▢ To control engine temperature

**2. How often should you check your vehicle's battery terminals for corrosion?**

A. ▢ Every month

B. ▢ Every 6 months

C. ▢ Every year

D. ▢ Only if the battery fails to start the vehicle

**3. What is the purpose of the vehicle's brake pads?**

A. ▢ To reduce engine noise

B. ▢ To provide a smoother ride

C. ▢ To assist with steering and maneuverability

D. ▢ To create friction and stop the vehicle

**4. When should you replace your vehicle's cabin air filter?**

A. ▢ Every 10,000 miles

B. ▢ Every year

C. ▢ Every 3 years

D. ▢ Only if there is a noticeable decrease in air quality

**5. What is the purpose of the vehicle's power windows?**

A. ▢ To enhance fuel efficiency

B. ▢ To regulate tire pressure

C. ▢ To provide occupant comfort and convenience

D. ▢ To control engine temperature


**6. How often should you check your vehicle's transmission fluid level?**

A. ▢ Every month

B. ▢ Every 3 months

C. ▢ Every 6 months

D. ▢ Only if you notice a decrease in performance or shifting issues


**7. What should you do if your vehicle's tire tread depth is below the recommended level?**

A. ▢ Ignore it as it does not affect safety

B. ▢ Inflate the tires to a higher pressure

C. ▢ Replace the tires immediately

D. ▢ Rotate the tires for better wear


**8. What is the purpose of the vehicle's airbags?**

A. ▢ To regulate tire pressure

B. ▢ To reduce engine noise

C. ▢ To provide occupant protection in a collision

D. ▢ To control engine temperature

**9. How often should you replace your vehicle's fuel filter?**

A. ▢ Every 20,000 miles

B. ▢ Every 50,000 miles

C. ▢ Every 100,000 miles

D. ▢ Only if it becomes clogged or damaged

**10. What is the purpose of the vehicle's ignition system?**

A. ▢ To control engine temperature

B. ▢ To enhance fuel efficiency

C. ▢ To regulate tire pressure

D. ▢ To provide a spark for engine combustion

**11. When should you replace your vehicle's timing belt?**

A. ▢ Every 50,000 miles

B. ▢ Every 75,000 miles

C. ▢ Every 100,000 miles

D. ▢ Only if it shows signs of wear or damage

**12. What should you do if your vehicle's turn signals are not functioning?**

A. ▢ Ignore it as it is not a safety concern

B. ▢ Use hand signals instead

C. ▢ Have the electrical system checked and repaired

D. ▢ Increase the volume of the vehicle's horn

**13. How often should you check your vehicle's power steering fluid level?**

A. ▢ Every month

B. ▢ Every 3 months

C. ▢ Every 6 months

D. ▢ Only if you notice a decrease in steering performance

**14. What is the purpose of the vehicle's exhaust system?**

A. ▢ To enhance fuel efficiency

B. ▢ To regulate tire pressure

C. ▢ To reduce noise from the engine

D. ▢ To safely remove exhaust gases from the engine

**15. How often should you replace your vehicle's spark plugs?**

A. ▢ Every 20,000 miles

B. ▢ Every 50,000 miles

C. ▢ Every 100,000 miles

D. ▢ Only if they show signs of wear or misfiring

# Correct answers for vehicle equipment and maintenance exam 4

**1. C.** To cool the engine

**2. A.** Every month

**3. D**. To create friction and stop the vehicle

**4. B**. Every year

**5. C.** To provide occupant comfort and convenience

**6. B.** Every 3 months

**7. C.** Replace the tires immediately

**8. C.** To provide occupant protection in a collision

**9. D.** Only if it becomes clogged or damaged

**10. D**. To provide a spark for engine combustion

**11. C.** Every 100,000 miles

**12. C.** Have the electrical system checked and repaired

**13. A.** Every month

**14. D.** To safely remove exhaust gases from the engine

**15. B.** Every 50,000 miles

# Vehicle equipment and maintenance exam 5

### 1. What is the purpose of the vehicle's alternator?

A. ▢ To regulate tire pressure

B. ▢ To provide power to the electrical system

C. ▢ To cool the engine

D. ▢ To control engine temperature

### 2. How often should you check your vehicle's engine oil level?

A. ▢ Every month

B. ▢ Every 6 months

C. ▢ Every year

D. ▢ Only if there is an oil leak

### 3. What is the purpose of the vehicle's suspension system?

A. ▢ To reduce engine noise

B. ▢ To provide a smoother ride

C. ▢ To assist with steering and maneuverability

D. ▢ To create friction and stop the vehicle

### 4. When should you replace your vehicle's windshield wiper blades?

A. ▢ Every 10,000 miles

B. ▢ Every year

C. ▢ Every 3 years

D. ▢ Only if they are torn or streaking

**5. What is the purpose of the vehicle's air conditioning system?**

A. ▢ To enhance fuel efficiency

B. ▢ To regulate tire pressure

C. ▢ To provide occupant comfort and temperature control

D. ▢ To control engine temperature

**6. How often should you check your vehicle's brake fluid level?**

A. ▢ Every month

B. ▢ Every 3 months

C. ▢ Every 6 months

D. ▢ Only if you notice a decrease in braking performance

**7. What should you do if your vehicle's headlights are dim or not working?**

A. ▢ Ignore it as it does not affect safety

B. ▢ Increase the brightness on the dashboard display

C. ▢ Replace the bulbs immediately

D. ▢ Use high beams instead

**8. What is the purpose of the vehicle's seat belts?**

A. ▢ To regulate tire pressure

B. ▢ To reduce engine noise

C. ▢ To provide occupant protection in a collision

D. ▢ To control engine temperature

**9. How often should you replace your vehicle's engine air filter?**

A. ▢ Every 20,000 miles

B. ▢ Every 50,000 miles

C. ▢ Every 100,000 miles

   D. ▢ Only if it becomes clogged or dirty

**10. What is the purpose of the vehicle's fuel system?**

A. ▢ To control engine temperature

B. ▢ To enhance fuel efficiency

C. ▢ To regulate tire pressure

D. ▢ To deliver fuel to the engine for combustion

**11. When should you replace your vehicle's serpentine belt?**

A. ▢ Every 50,000 miles

B. ▢ Every 75,000 miles

C. ▢ Every 100,000 miles

D. ▢ Only if it shows signs of wear or damage

**12. What should you do if your vehicle's horn is not functioning?**

A. ▢ Ignore it as it is not a safety concern

B. ▢ Use hand signals instead

C. ▢ Have the electrical system checked and repaired

D. ▢ Increase the volume of the vehicle's radio

**13. How often should you check your vehicle's tire pressure?**

A. ▢ Every month

B. ▢ Every 3 months

C. ▢ Every 6 months

D. ▢ Only if you notice a decrease in handling or tire wear

**14. What is the purpose of the vehicle's exhaust system?**

A. ▢ To enhance fuel efficiency

B. ▢ To regulate tire pressure

C. ▢ To reduce noise from the engine

D. ▢ To safely remove exhaust gases from the engine

**15. How often should you replace your vehicle's cabin air filter?**

A. ▢ Every 20,000 miles

B. ▢ Every 50,000 miles

C. ▢ Every 100,000 miles

D. ▢ Only if it becomes clogged or dirty

# Correct answers for vehicle equipment and maintenance exam 5

**1. B.** To provide power to the electrical system

**2. A.** Every month

**3. B**. To provide a smoother ride

**4. D**. Only if they are torn or streaking

**5. C.** To provide occupant comfort and temperature control

**6. A.** Every month

**7. C**. Replace the bulbs immediately

**8. C**. To provide occupant protection in a collision

**9. D.** Only if it becomes clogged or dirty

**10. D.** To deliver fuel to the engine for combustion

**11. C.** Every 100,000 miles

**12. C**. Have the electrical system checked and repaired

**13. A.** Every month

**14. D.** To safely remove exhaust gases from the engine

**15. D**. Only if it becomes clogged or dirty

# Sharing the road

Welcome to Chapter 5 of the Minnesota DMV Exam Workbook, where we explore the vital topic of sharing the road. In this chapter, we will delve into the principles of sharing the road with other drivers, pedestrians, cyclists, and various road users. Understanding the rules, responsibilities, and best practices for sharing the road is essential for creating a harmonious and safe road environment in the Land of 10,000 Lakes.

Sharing the road is a fundamental aspect of responsible and courteous driving. This section will emphasize the significance of sharing the road with other road users, highlighting the importance of respect, patience, and cooperation. By recognizing the diverse mix of vehicles, pedestrians, and cyclists on Minnesota's roads, we can foster a culture of inclusivity and safety.

## Rules and Responsibilities

This section will provide an overview of the rules and responsibilities associated with sharing the road. We will explore traffic laws, right-of-way principles, and the importance of adhering to road signs, signals, and markings. Understanding and following these rules and responsibilities are crucial for maintaining order and preventing conflicts on the road.

## Interacting with Pedestrians

Pedestrians play a significant role in the road ecosystem, and it is essential to understand their needs and rights. This section will discuss the importance of yielding to pedestrians, especially at crosswalks and intersections. We will also explore techniques for anticipating and responding to pedestrian behavior, such as making eye contact and adjusting speed when approaching pedestrian-heavy areas.

## Sharing the Road with Cyclists

Cyclists are an increasingly common sight on Minnesota's roads, and sharing the road with them requires special consideration. This section will focus on the principles of sharing the road with cyclists, including providing adequate space when passing, being mindful of their vulnerability, and recognizing their right to use the road. We will also discuss common cycling hand signals and how to interact safely with cyclists in various traffic scenarios.

## Sharing the Road with Motorcyclists

Motorcyclists have specific needs and vulnerabilities on the road, and it is crucial to be mindful of their presence. This section will explore best practices for sharing the road with motorcyclists, such as giving them ample space, being cautious at intersections, and checking blind spots carefully. We will discuss the importance of communication and awareness to enhance the safety of both motorcyclists and other road users.

## Sharing the Road with Commercial Vehicles

Commercial vehicles, such as trucks and buses, have unique characteristics and limitations that require special attention. This section will highlight the importance of sharing the road safely with commercial vehicles, including avoiding their blind spots, maintaining a safe following distance, and being patient when they maneuver or make turns. Understanding how to interact with commercial vehicles can prevent accidents and ensure the smooth flow of traffic.

## Work Zones and Construction Areas

Navigating through work zones and construction areas requires heightened caution and adherence to specific guidelines. This section will discuss the challenges posed by work zones and the importance of reducing speed, following detour signs, and being mindful of construction workers.

We will emphasize the significance of planning ahead and allowing extra time to navigate through these areas safely.

## School Zones and School Buses

The safety of children is paramount, especially in school zones and around school buses. This section will provide guidance on safely sharing the road in school zones, including reduced speed limits, yielding to pedestrians, and being cautious around school buses. We will discuss the legal requirements for stopping for school buses and the potential consequences of violating these rules.

## Sharing the Road in Inclement Weather

Inclement weather conditions require extra caution and adjustment of driving behavior. This section will focus on the principles of sharing the road in adverse weather, such as rain, snow, and fog. We will explore strategies for maintaining safe distances, adjusting speed, and using appropriate vehicle equipment to enhance traction and visibility.

## Conclusion

By understanding the principles of sharing the road, you are taking active steps towards promoting safety and cooperation on Minnesota's roads. Throughout this chapter, we will delve deeper into the specific aspects of sharing the road, providing you with the knowledge and skills necessary to navigate diverse road scenarios and foster a culture of respect and safety. So, let's embark on this journey of shared responsibility, ensuring a safer and more harmonious road environment for all who travel through the Land of 10,000 Lakes.

For training purposes, you can mark the ▢ symbol next to what you think is the correct answer: Once you  have chosen the correct answer, use a pencil or pen to mark the ▢ symbol next to that answer.

# Sharing the road exam

**1. When approaching a pedestrian crossing at an intersection, you should:**

A. ▢  Stop and yield to pedestrians in the crosswalk

B. ▢  Honk your horn to alert pedestrians of your presence

C. ▢  Speed up to cross the intersection quickly

D. ▢  Slow down and proceed with caution

**2. What should you do when sharing the road with a bicyclist?**

A. ▢  Maintain a safe distance and pass when it's safe to do so

B. ▢  Drive closely behind the bicyclist to provide protection

C. ▢  Honk your horn to let the bicyclist know you're nearby

D. ▢  Drive in the bicycle lane to avoid traffic congestion

**3. What does a solid yellow line on the roadway indicate?**

A. ▢  No passing allowed in either direction

B. ▢  Passing allowed on the right side only

C. ▢  Passing allowed on the left side only

D. ▢  No passing allowed on the left side only

**4. When approaching a school bus with its red lights flashing and stop arm extended, you should:**

A. ▢  Speed up and pass the school bus quickly

B. ▢  Stop and wait until the lights stop flashing and the stop arm is retracted

C. ○ Drive around the school bus on the left side

D. ○ Slow down and proceed with caution

**5. What should you do when you encounter an emergency vehicle with its lights and sirens activated?**

A. ○ Speed up to clear the way for the emergency vehicle

B. ○ Pull over to the right side of the road and stop until the emergency vehicle passes

C. ○ Continue driving without changing your speed or direction

D. ○ Follow closely behind the emergency vehicle to maintain traffic flow

**6. What is the speed limit in a school zone when children are present?**

A. ○ 25 mph

B. ○ 35 mph

C. ○ 45 mph

D. ○ 55 mph

**7. When should you use your horn while sharing the road with other drivers?**

A. ○ To signal your frustration with other drivers' behavior

B. ○ To alert others of your presence when necessary to avoid a collision

C. ○ To greet friends or acquaintances on the road

D. ○ To communicate your disagreement with other drivers' decisions

**8. What should you do when you approach a roundabout?**

A. ○ Speed up to merge into traffic smoothly

B. ○ Yield to traffic already in the roundabout and enter when it's safe to do so

C. ○ Stop and wait for all vehicles in the roundabout to exit before entering

D. ○ Drive against the flow of traffic to exit the roundabout quickly

**9. When are you required to yield the right-of-way to pedestrians?**

A. ▢ Only when pedestrians are crossing at marked crosswalks

B. ▢ Only when pedestrians are using a designated pedestrian bridge

C. ▢ Always, whether or not there is a marked crosswalk

D. ▢ Only when pedestrians are walking on the sidewalk

**10. What does a yellow diamond-shaped sign with black symbols indicate?**

A. ▢ Railroad crossing ahead

B. ▢ Intersection ahead

C. ▢ Road work ahead

D. ▢ Yield sign ahead

**11. What should you do when approaching a funeral procession?**

A. ▢ Follow closely behind the procession to maintain traffic flow

B. ▢ Yield the right-of-way to the entire procession and wait until it has passed

C. ▢ Pass the procession quickly to avoid being delayed

D. ▢ Honk your horn to express condolences

**12. What should you do when you approach a yield sign?**

A. ▢ Speed up to merge into traffic without stopping

B. ▢ Stop and wait for a gap in traffic before proceeding

C. ▢ Ignore the yield sign if there is no traffic coming

D. ▢ Yield the right-of-way to traffic already in the intersection

**13. What is the purpose of a regulatory sign?**

A. ▢ To provide information about points of interest

B. ▢ To indicate recommended driving speeds

C. ▢ To provide guidance and enforce traffic rules

D. ▢ To warn drivers about potential hazards ahead

**14. What does a red and white triangular sign indicate?**

A. ▢ Yield ahead

B. ▢ Stop ahead

C. ▢ Speed limit ahead

D. ▢ Railroad crossing ahead

**15. When are you allowed to pass another vehicle on the right side?**

A. ▢ When the vehicle ahead is making a left turn

B. ▢ When the vehicle ahead is traveling below the speed limit

C. ▢ When there is a solid yellow line on your side of the roadway

D. ▢ When there is heavy traffic in the left lane

## Correct answers for sharing the road exam

**1. A.** Stop and yield to pedestrians in the crosswalk

**2. A.** Maintain a safe distance and pass when it's safe to do so

**3. A.** No passing allowed in either direction

**4. B.** Stop and wait until the lights stop flashing and the stop arm is retracted

**5. B.** Pull over to the right side of the road and stop until the emergency vehicle passes

**6. A.** 25 mph

**7. B.** To alert others of your presence when necessary to avoid a collision

**8. B.** Yield to traffic already in the roundabout and enter when it's safe to do so

**9. C.** Always, whether or not there is a marked crosswalk

**10. A.** Railroad crossing ahead

**11. B.** Yield the right-of-way to the entire procession and wait until it has passed

**12. B.** Stop and wait for a gap in traffic before proceeding

**13. C.** To provide guidance and enforce traffic rules

**14. A.** Yield ahead

**15. A.** When the vehicle ahead is making a left turn

# Sharing the road exam 2

**1. When sharing the road with motorcycles, you should:**

A. ▢ Maintain a safe following distance

B. ▢ Drive closely behind them to provide protection

C. ▢ Honk your horn to alert them of your presence

D. ▢ Pass them quickly on the right side

**2. What should you do when you see a pedestrian using a white cane at a crosswalk?**

A. ▢ Stop and yield the right-of-way to the pedestrian

B. ▢ Flash your headlights to warn the pedestrian

C. ▢ Proceed through the crosswalk quickly to avoid delays

D. ▢ Honk your horn to let the pedestrian know you're approaching

**3. What is the purpose of a shared center turn lane?**

A. ▢ To allow vehicles to make left turns from either direction

B. ▢ To provide an additional travel lane for vehicles

C. ▢ To park vehicles temporarily during peak hours

D. ▢ To provide a space for emergency vehicle parking

**4. What should you do when a bicyclist is occupying the travel lane ahead of you?**

A. ▢ Honk your horn to signal them to move to the side

B. ▢ Wait patiently until it is safe to pass in an adjacent lane

C. ▢ Flash your high beams to indicate your presence

D. ▢ Drive as close as possible to the bicyclist to pass quickly

**5. When approaching a blind pedestrian who is using a guide dog or white cane, you should:**

A. ▢ Stop and wait for the pedestrian to cross the street

B. ▢ Slow down and proceed with caution

C. ▢ Pass the pedestrian quickly to avoid delays

D. ▢ Honk your horn to alert the pedestrian of your presence

**6. What should you do when approaching a bicyclist from behind?**

A. ▢ Maintain a safe distance and pass when it's safe to do so

B. ▢ Drive closely behind them to provide protection

C. ▢ Honk your horn to let them know you're approaching

D. ▢ Pass them quickly on the left side

**7. What should you do when approaching a stopped school bus with its red lights flashing and stop arm extended?**

A. ▢ Stop and wait until the lights stop flashing and the stop arm is retracted

B. ▢ Slow down and proceed with caution

C. ▢ Pass the school bus quickly on the right side

D. ▢ Honk your horn to alert the children to move away from the bus

**8. When passing a bicyclist, you should leave a minimum of _____ of space between your vehicle and the bicycle.**

A. ▢ Three feet

B. ▢ Four feet

C. ▢ Five feet

D. ▢ Six feet

**9. What should you do when approaching a construction zone?**

A. ▢ Reduce your speed and follow the signs and signals

B. ▢ Speed up to get through the zone quickly

C. ▢ Use your high beams to improve visibility

D. ▢ Ignore the construction signs and continue at the same speed


**10. When approaching a roundabout, you should:**

A. ▢ Yield to traffic already in the roundabout and enter when it's safe to do so

B. ▢ Speed up to merge into traffic smoothly

C. ▢ Stop and wait for all vehicles in the roundabout to exit before entering

D. ▢ Drive against the flow of traffic to exit quickly


**11. When passing a pedestrian, you should:**

A. ▢ Slow down and give them plenty of space

B. ▢ Drive closely behind them to guide their movement

C. ▢ Honk your horn to alert them of your presence

D. ▢ Pass quickly on the right side to avoid delays


**12. What should you do when you see a bicyclist using a hand signal to indicate a left turn?**

A. ▢ Yield the right-of-way and allow them to turn safely

B. ▢ Speed up to pass them before they turn

C. ▢ Honk your horn to let them know you're approaching

D. ▢ Ignore the hand signal and continue driving

**13. What should you do when approaching a crosswalk with pedestrians present?**

A. ▢ Stop and yield the right-of-way to the pedestrians

B. ▢ Maintain your speed and proceed through the crosswalk quickly

C. ▢ Honk your horn to alert the pedestrians of your presence

D. ▢ Slow down slightly, but proceed if the pedestrians are far enough away

**14. When sharing the road with large trucks or buses, you should:**

A. ▢ Avoid driving in their blind spots or "no-zones"

B. ▢ Tailgate closely behind them to improve visibility

C. ▢ Pass them quickly on the right side

D. ▢ Flash your high beams to let them know you're passing

**15. What should you do when sharing the road with motorcycles?**

A. ▢ Be aware of their presence and give them space

B. ▢ Drive closely behind them to provide protection

C. ▢ Pass them quickly on the left side

D. ▢ Honk your horn to signal them to move over

# Correct answers for sharing the road exam 2

**1. A.** Maintain a safe following distance

**2. A.** Stop and yield the right-of-way to the pedestrian

**3. A.** To allow vehicles to make left turns from either direction

**4. B.** Wait patiently until it is safe to pass in an adjacent lane

**5. B.** Slow down and proceed with caution

**6. A.** Maintain a safe distance and pass when it's safe to do so

**7. A.** Stop and wait until the lights stop flashing and the stop arm is retracted

**8. A.** Three feet

**9. A.** Reduce your speed and follow the signs and signals

**10. A.** Yield to traffic already in the roundabout and enter when it's safe to do so

**11. A.** Slow down and give them plenty of space

**12. A.** Yield the right-of-way and allow them to turn safely

**13. A.** Stop and yield the right-of-way to the pedestrians

**14. A.** Avoid driving in their blind spots or "no-zones"

**15. A.** Be aware of their presence and give them space

## Sharing the road exam 3

**1. When approaching a bicycle lane, you should:**

A. ▢ Drive in the bicycle lane to avoid traffic congestion

B. ▢ Merge into the bicycle lane before making a turn

C. ▢ Yield to bicycles in the bicycle lane before crossing it

D. ▢ Honk your horn to alert cyclists of your presence

**2. What should you do when approaching a pedestrian crossing the road at a marked crosswalk?**

A. ▢ Stop and yield the right-of-way to the pedestrian

B. ▢ Speed up to pass the pedestrian quickly

C. ▢ Flash your high beams to signal the pedestrian to cross

D. ▢ Honk your horn to warn the pedestrian of your presence

**3. When sharing the road with motorcyclists, you should:**

A. ▢ Give them extra space and maintain a safe following distance

B. ▢ Tailgate closely behind them for improved visibility

C. ▢ Pass them quickly on the right side

D. ▢ Use your high beams to signal them to move over

**4. What should you do when encountering an emergency vehicle with its lights and sirens activated?**

A. ▢ Yield the right-of-way and move to the right side of the road

B. ▢ Speed up to get out of the way quickly

C. ▢ Continue driving at the same speed and ignore the emergency vehicle

D. ▢ Flash your headlights to alert the emergency vehicle of your presence

**5. When approaching a stopped school bus with its red lights flashing and stop arm extended on a divided highway with a median strip, you should:**

A. ▢ Stop if you are traveling in the same direction as the bus

B. ▢ Slow down and proceed with caution

C. ▢ Pass the bus quickly on the right side

D. ▢ Honk your horn to alert the children to move away from the bus

**6. What should you do when encountering a pedestrian using a wheelchair or mobility device on a sidewalk?**

A. ▢ Yield the right-of-way and allow them to continue

B. ▢ Drive on the sidewalk to pass them

C. ▢ Honk your horn to alert them of your presence

D. ▢ Continue driving without slowing down

**7. What should you do when approaching a yield sign?**

A. ▢ Slow down and be prepared to stop if necessary

B. ▢ Speed up and merge into traffic quickly

C. ▢ Ignore the yield sign and proceed without stopping

D. ▢ Honk your horn to signal other drivers to yield to you

**8. When sharing the road with pedestrians, you should:**

A. ▢ Be attentive and yield the right-of-way when necessary

B. ▢ Drive closely behind them to guide their movement

C. ▢ Pass them quickly on the left side

D. ▢ Use your high beams to improve their visibility

**9. What should you do when approaching a construction zone with flaggers?**

A. ▢ Obey the instructions given by the flaggers

B. ▢ Drive through the construction zone at the same speed

C. ▢ Ignore the flaggers and continue driving

D. ▢ Flash your headlights to signal the flaggers to let you through

**10. When passing a bicyclist, you should leave a minimum of _____ of space between your vehicle and the bicycle.**

A. ▢ Two feet

B. ▢ Three feet

C. ▢ Four feet

D. ▢ Five feet

**11. What should you do when approaching a pedestrian crossing at an unmarked crosswalk?**

A. ▢ Yield the right-of-way and allow the pedestrian to cross

B. ▢ Speed up to pass the pedestrian quickly

C. ▢ Sound your horn to alert the pedestrian of your presence

D. ▢ Ignore the pedestrian and continue driving

**12. When sharing the road with a large commercial truck, you should:**

A. ▢ Avoid driving in their blind spots or "no-zones"

B. ▢ Tailgate closely behind the truck for better visibility

C. ▢ Pass the truck quickly on the right side

D. ▢ Flash your high beams to signal the truck to move over

**13. What should you do when encountering a funeral procession?**

A. ▢ Yield the right-of-way and show respect by not passing

B. ▢ Speed up to get through the procession quickly

C. ▢ Honk your horn to alert the mourners of your presence

D. ▢ Ignore the procession and continue driving as usual

**14. When approaching a pedestrian walking with a white cane or guide dog, you should:**

A. ▢ Yield the right-of-way and exercise caution

B. ▢ Drive closely behind them for guidance

C. ▢ Pass them quickly on the left side

D. ▢ Flash your high beams to get their attention

**15. What should you do when approaching a roundabout?**

A. ▢ Yield to traffic already in the roundabout and enter when it's safe to do so

B. ▢ Speed up to enter the roundabout before other vehicles

C. ▢ Honk your horn to alert other drivers of your presence

D. ▢ Drive through the roundabout in the opposite direction

## Correct answers for sharing the road exam 3

**1. C.** Yield to bicycles in the bicycle lane before crossing it

**2. A**. Stop and yield the right-of-way to the pedestrian

**3. A**. Give them extra space and maintain a safe following distance

**4. A.** Yield the right-of-way and move to the right side of the road

**5. A.** Stop if you are traveling in the same direction as the bus

**6. A.** Yield the right-of-way and allow them to continue

**7. A.** Slow down and be prepared to stop if necessary

**8. A.** Be attentive and yield the right-of-way when necessary

**9. A.** Obey the instructions given by the flaggers

**10. B.** Three feet

**11. A.** Yield the right-of-way and allow the pedestrian to cross

**12. A.** Avoid driving in their blind spots or "no-zones"

**13. A.** Yield the right-of-way and show respect by not passing

**14. A.** Yield the right-of-way and exercise caution

**15. A.** Yield to traffic already in the roundabout and enter when it's safe to do so

## Sharing the road exam 4

**1. When driving on a road with a bike lane, you should:**

A. ▢ Use the bike lane as an additional driving lane

B. ▢ Merge into the bike lane when making a turn

C. ▢ Yield to bicyclists before crossing the bike lane

D. ▢ Honk your horn to alert bicyclists of your presence

**2. What should you do when approaching a pedestrian crossing the road at an unmarked crosswalk?**

A. ▢ Stop and yield the right-of-way to the pedestrian

B. ▢ Increase your speed to pass the pedestrian quickly

C. ▢ Flash your high beams to signal the pedestrian to cross

D. ▢ Honk your horn to warn the pedestrian of your presence

**3. When sharing the road with motorcycles, you should:**

A. ▢ Give them extra space and maintain a safe following distance

B. ▢ Tailgate closely behind them for improved visibility

C. ▢ Pass them quickly on the right side

D. ▢ Use your high beams to signal them to move over

**4. What should you do when you see an emergency vehicle approaching from behind with lights and sirens activated?**

A. ▢ Yield the right-of-way and move to the right side of the road

B. ▢ Increase your speed to create a gap for the emergency vehicle

C. ▢ Continue driving at the same speed and ignore the emergency vehicle

D. ▢ Flash your headlights to signal the emergency vehicle to pass

**5. When approaching a stopped school bus with its red lights flashing and stop arm extended on a two-lane road, you should:**

A. ▢ Stop and remain stopped until the bus resumes motion

B. ▢ Slow down and proceed with caution if there are no children around

C. ▢ Pass the bus quickly on the right side

D. ▢ Honk your horn to alert the children to stay away from the bus

**6. What should you do when you encounter a pedestrian using a white cane or guide dog?**

A. ▢ Yield the right-of-way and allow them to cross safely

B. ▢ Drive around them on the sidewalk to avoid delays

C. ▢ Honk your horn to alert them of your presence

D. ▢ Continue driving without slowing down

**7. What should you do when approaching a yield sign?**

A. ▢ Slow down and be prepared to stop if necessary

B. ▢ Speed up and merge into traffic quickly

C. ▢ Ignore the yield sign and proceed without stopping

D. ▢ Honk your horn to signal other drivers to yield to you

**8. When sharing the road with pedestrians, you should:**

A. ▢ Be attentive and yield the right-of-way when necessary

B. ▢ Drive closely behind them to guide their movement

C. ▢ Pass them quickly on the left side

D. ▢ Use your high beams to improve their visibility

**9. What should you do when approaching a construction zone with flaggers directing traffic?**

A. ▢ Obey the instructions given by the flaggers

B. ▢ Drive through the construction zone at the same speed

C. ▢ Ignore the flaggers and continue driving

D. ▢ Flash your headlights to signal the flaggers to let you through

**10. When passing a bicyclist, you should leave a minimum of _____ of space between your vehicle and the bicycle.**

A. ▢ Two feet

B. ▢ Three feet

C. ▢ Four feet

D. ▢ Five feet

**11. What should you do when approaching a pedestrian crossing at an unmarked crosswalk?**

A. ▢ Yield the right-of-way and allow the pedestrian to cross

B. ▢ Speed up to pass the pedestrian quickly

C. ▢ Sound your horn to alert the pedestrian of your presence

D. ▢ Ignore the pedestrian and continue driving

**12. When sharing the road with a large commercial truck, you should:**

A. ▢ Avoid driving in their blind spots or "no-zones"

B. ▢ Tailgate closely behind the truck for better visibility

C. ▢ Pass the truck quickly on the right side

D. ▢ Flash your high beams to signal the truck to move over

**13. What should you do when encountering a funeral procession?**

A. ▢ Yield the right-of-way and show respect by not passing

B. ▢ Speed up to get through the procession quickly

C. ▢ Honk your horn to alert the mourners of your presence

D. ▢ Ignore the procession and continue driving as usual

**14. When approaching a pedestrian walking with a white cane or guide dog, you should:**

A. ▢ Yield the right-of-way and exercise caution

B. ▢ Drive closely behind them for guidance

C. ▢ Pass them quickly on the left side

D. ▢ Flash your high beams to get their attention

**15. What should you do when approaching a roundabout?**

A. ▢ Yield to traffic already in the roundabout and enter when it's safe to do so

B. ▢ Speed up to enter the roundabout before other vehicles

C. ▢ Honk your horn to alert other drivers of your presence

D. ▢ Drive through the roundabout in the opposite direction

# Correct answers for sharing the road exam 4

**1. C.** Yield to bicyclists before crossing the bike lane

**2. A.** Stop and yield the right-of-way to the pedestrian

**3. A.** Give them extra space and maintain a safe following distance

**4. A.** Yield the right-of-way and move to the right side of the road

**5. A.** Stop if you are traveling in the same direction as the bus

**6. A.** Yield the right-of-way and allow them to continue

**7. A.** Slow down and be prepared to stop if necessary

**8. A.** Be attentive and yield the right-of-way when necessary

**9. A**. Obey the instructions given by the flaggers

**10. B**. Three feet

**11. A**. Yield the right-of-way and allow the pedestrian to cross

**12. A.** Avoid driving in their blind spots or "no-zones"

**13. A.** Yield the right-of-way and show respect by not passing

**14. A.** Yield the right-of-way and exercise caution

**15. A.** Yield to traffic already in the roundabout and enter when it's safe to do so

## Sharing the road exam 5

**1. When approaching a pedestrian crosswalk, you should:**

A. ▢ Speed up to pass the pedestrian quickly

B. ▢ Stop and yield the right-of-way to the pedestrian

C. ▢ Flash your headlights to signal the pedestrian to cross

D. ▢ Honk your horn to alert the pedestrian of your presence

**2. What should you do when sharing the road with large trucks or buses?**

A. ▢ Stay out of their blind spots or "no-zones"

B. ▢ Tailgate closely behind them for better visibility

C. ▢ Pass them quickly on the right side

D. ▢ Use your high beams to signal them to move over

**3. When approaching a railroad crossing with flashing lights, you should:**

A. ▢ Speed up and try to cross before the train arrives

B. ▢ Stop and wait for the train to pass completely

C. ▢ Proceed with caution and cross the tracks slowly

D. ▢ Honk your horn to alert the train engineer of your presence

**4. What should you do when approaching a stopped emergency vehicle with its lights activated?**

A. ▢ Slow down and move over to a non-adjacent lane if possible

B. ▢ Increase your speed to pass the emergency vehicle quickly

C. ▢ Ignore the emergency vehicle and continue driving

D. ▢ Flash your high beams to warn other drivers of the emergency vehicle

**5. When sharing the road with bicycles, you should:**

A. ▢ Give them at least three feet of space when passing

B. ▢ Tailgate closely behind them for better visibility

C. ▢ Pass them quickly on the right side

D. ▢ Use your high beams to signal them to move over

**6. What should you do when encountering a funeral procession?**

A. ▢ Yield the right-of-way and show respect by not passing

B. ▢ Speed up to get through the procession quickly

C. ▢ Honk your horn to alert the mourners of your presence

D. ▢ Ignore the procession and continue driving as usual

**7. When approaching a construction zone with workers present, you should:**

A. ▢ Slow down and follow any posted detour or lane closure signs

B. ▢ Speed up to get through the construction zone quickly

C. ▢ Ignore the construction workers and continue driving

D. ▢ Flash your headlights to signal the workers to let you through

**8. What should you do when approaching a school bus with flashing red lights and an extended stop arm on a divided highway?**

A. ▢ Stop if you are traveling in the same direction as the bus

B. ▢ Slow down and proceed with caution if there are no children around

C. ▢ Pass the bus quickly on the left side

D. ▢ Honk your horn to alert the children to stay away from the bus

**9. When sharing the road with motorcyclists, you should:**

A. ▢ Give them extra space and maintain a safe following distance

B. ▢ Tailgate closely behind them for better visibility

C. ▢ Pass them quickly on the right side

D. ▢ Use your high beams to signal them to move over

**10. What should you do when approaching a pedestrian walking with a white cane or guide dog?**

A. ▢ Yield the right-of-way and allow them to continue

B. ▢ Drive closely behind them for guidance

C. ▢ Pass them quickly on the left side

D. ▢ Flash your high beams to get their attention

**11. When approaching a roundabout, you should:**

A. ▢ Yield to traffic already in the roundabout and enter when it's safe to do so

B. ▢ Speed up to enter the roundabout before other vehicles

C. ▢ Honk your horn to alert other drivers of your presence

D. ▢ Drive through the roundabout in the opposite direction

**12. What should you do when encountering a bicyclist on the road?**

A. ▢ Be attentive and yield the right-of-way when necessary

B. ▢ Tailgate closely behind them for better visibility

C. ▢ Pass them quickly on the right side

D. ▢ Flash your high beams to signal them to move over

**13. When sharing the road with pedestrians, you should:**

A. ▢ Yield the right-of-way and exercise caution

B. ▢ Tailgate closely behind them for better visibility

C. ▢ Pass them quickly on the right side

D. ▢ Use your high beams to signal them to move over

**14. What should you do when approaching a bicyclist in a bike lane?**

A. ▢ Give them at least three feet of space when passing

B. ▢ Tailgate closely behind them for better visibility

C. ▢ Pass them quickly on the right side

D. ▢ Use your high beams to signal them to move over

**15. When sharing the road with motorcyclists, you should:**

A. ▢ Give them extra space and maintain a safe following distance

B. ▢ Tailgate closely behind them for better visibility

C. ▢ Pass them quickly on the right side

D. ▢ Use your high beams to signal them to move over

# Correct answers for sharing the road exam 5

**1. B.** Stop and yield the right-of-way to the pedestrian

**2. A**. Stay out of their blind spots or "no-zones"

**3. B**. Stop and wait for the train to pass completely

**4. A.** Slow down and move over to a non-adjacent lane if possible

**5. A.** Give them at least three feet of space when passing

**6. A.** Yield the right-of-way and show respect by not passing

**7. A**. Slow down and follow any posted detour or lane closure signs

**8. A.** Stop if you are traveling in the same direction as the bus

**9. A.** Give them extra space and maintain a safe following distance

**10. A.** Yield the right-of-way and allow them to continue

**11. A.** Yield to traffic already in the roundabout and enter when it's safe to do so

**12. A.** Be attentive and yield the right-of-way when necessary

**13. A.** Yield the right-of-way and exercise caution

**14. A.** Give them at least three feet of space when passing

**15. A.** Give them extra space and maintain a safe following distance

# Transportation of hazardous materials

Welcome to Chapter 6 of the Minnesota DMV Exam Workbook, where we explore the critical topic of transporting hazardous materials. In this chapter, we will delve into the regulations, responsibilities, and best practices associated with the transportation of hazardous materials. Understanding the risks, proper handling procedures, and safety precautions related to hazardous materials is crucial for safeguarding our communities and the environment.

Transporting hazardous materials presents unique challenges and potential risks. This section will emphasize the importance of safe transportation practices, highlighting the potential hazards associated with these materials. By adhering to regulations and implementing proper handling and storage procedures, we can mitigate risks and ensure the safety of ourselves and others on the road.

## Regulatory Framework for Transportation of Hazardous Materials

Transporting hazardous materials is governed by a comprehensive regulatory framework to ensure safety and compliance. This section will provide an overview of the federal and state regulations that govern the transportation of hazardous materials in Minnesota. We will explore the roles and responsibilities of different entities involved in the transportation process, such as shippers, carriers, and drivers.

## Classifying and Identifying Hazardous Materials

Hazardous materials are classified based on their potential risks and properties. This section will delve into the different hazard classes and divisions, as defined by the Hazardous Materials Regulations (HMR). We will explore the proper labeling, marking, and placarding requirements to accurately identify and communicate the nature of the hazardous materials being transported.

## Packaging and Handling Hazardous Materials

Proper packaging and handling of hazardous materials are essential to prevent leaks, spills, and potential accidents. This section will discuss the requirements for packaging materials, including containers, drums, and tanks, to ensure their integrity during transportation. We will also explore best practices for handling hazardous materials, including proper loading, securing, and unloading techniques.

## Documentation and Emergency Response Planning

Comprehensive documentation and emergency response planning are crucial for effective management of hazardous materials during transportation. This section will cover the necessary documentation, such as shipping papers and emergency response information, to accompany hazardous materials shipments. We will also discuss the importance of developing and implementing emergency response plans to address potential incidents and minimize their impact.

## Driver Training and Qualifications

Drivers involved in the transportation of hazardous materials must undergo specialized training and possess specific qualifications. This section will outline the training requirements, including general awareness, function-specific, and security awareness training. We will emphasize the importance of driver competence, awareness, and preparedness to handle hazardous materials safely and respond appropriately in emergency situations.

## Security Considerations

Transporting hazardous materials requires heightened security measures to prevent unauthorized access and potential malicious activities. This section will highlight the importance of maintaining security protocols, including proper vehicle inspections, cargo seals, and secure parking practices. We will explore strategies to enhance the security of hazardous materials shipments and reduce the risk of theft or tampering.

## Environmental Considerations

The transportation of hazardous materials has significant environmental implications. This section will discuss the importance of minimizing environmental impacts through spill prevention, proper waste disposal, and adherence to environmental regulations. We will emphasize the role of responsible practices in protecting Minnesota's natural resources and ecosystems.

## Conclusion

By understanding the complexities and best practices associated with the transportation of hazardous materials, you are taking proactive steps towards ensuring safety, security, and environmental protection in Minnesota. Throughout this chapter, we will delve deeper into the specific aspects of transporting hazardous materials, providing you with the knowledge and skills necessary to navigate the regulatory landscape and handle these materials safely. So, let's embark on this journey of responsible transportation, safeguarding our communities and the environment in the Land of 10,000 Lakes.

For training purposes, you can mark the ▢ symbol next to what you think is the correct answer: Once you have chosen the correct answer, use a pencil or pen to mark the ▢ symbol next to that answer.

# Transportation of hazardous materials exam

**1. When transporting hazardous materials, it is important to:**

A. ▢ Use caution and follow all regulations

B. ▢ Speed up to reach your destination quickly

C. ▢ Ignore any warning signs or labels

D. ▢ Drive during peak traffic hours to avoid inspections

**2. What is the purpose of placards on vehicles transporting hazardous materials?**

A. ▢ To alert others of the potential hazards

B. ▢ To indicate the vehicle's registration number

C. ▢ To promote a specific brand or company

D. ▢ To increase fuel efficiency

**3. Before transporting hazardous materials, you should:**

A. ▢ Obtain the necessary permits and certifications

B. ▢ Carry as much cargo as possible to maximize efficiency

C. ▢ Ignore any special handling instructions

D. ▢ Operate the vehicle at high speeds to reduce the risk of accidents

**4. What should you do if you witness a hazardous materials spill on the road?**

A. ▢ Stay clear of the area and notify the authorities

B. ▢ Attempt to clean up the spill yourself

C. ▢ Drive through the spill area as quickly as possible

D. ▢ Ignore the spill and continue driving as usual

**5. How should you handle a vehicle fire when transporting hazardous materials?**

A. ▫ Follow established emergency procedures and seek assistance

B. ▫ Attempt to extinguish the fire yourself

C. ▫ Drive faster to escape the fire's reach

D. ▫ Ignore the fire and continue driving to your destination

**6. What does the "Flammable" placard indicate on a vehicle transporting hazardous materials?**

A. ▫ The cargo being transported is highly combustible

B. ▫ The vehicle is carrying a large quantity of fuel

C. ▫ The vehicle is transporting fireworks

D. ▫ The driver is a certified firefighter

**7. When transporting hazardous materials, you should:**

A. ▫ Follow designated routes and avoid restricted areas

B. ▫ Take shortcuts to reach your destination faster

C. ▫ Disregard weight restrictions to carry more cargo

D. ▫ Ignore any warning signs or labels on the vehicle

**8. What should you do if you suspect a leak in the cargo you are transporting?**

A. ▫ Stop in a safe location and inspect for leaks

B. ▫ Drive faster to reach your destination quickly

C. ▫ Ignore the leak and continue driving as usual

D. ▫ Open the windows to ventilate the vehicle

**9. How should you handle a tire blowout when transporting hazardous materials?**

A. ○ Maintain control of the vehicle and safely pull over

B. ○ Continue driving at high speeds to avoid traffic congestion

C. ○ Ignore the blowout and continue driving to your destination

D. ○ Honk your horn to alert other drivers of the blowout

**10. What should you do if you are involved in an accident while transporting hazardous materials?**

A. ○ Notify the authorities and follow emergency procedures

B. ○ Attempt to hide the hazardous materials from inspection

C. ○ Leave the scene of the accident immediately

D. ○ Ignore the accident and continue driving to your destination

**11. What does the "Corrosive" placard indicate on a vehicle transporting hazardous materials?**

A. ○ The cargo has the potential to cause chemical burns or damage

B. ○ The vehicle is carrying radioactive materials

C. ○ The driver is transporting corrosive cleaning supplies

D. ○ The cargo is safe and non-hazardous

**12. How should you secure hazardous materials in your vehicle?**

A. ○ Use proper restraints and containers as specified by regulations

B. ○ Place the materials loosely in the back of the vehicle

C. ○ Ignore securing the materials to save time

D. ○ Stack the materials as high as possible to maximize space

**13. What should you do if you encounter a railroad crossing while transporting hazardous materials?**

A. ▢ Stop, look, and listen for approaching trains

B. ▢ Ignore the crossing and proceed without caution

C. ▢ Increase your speed to cross the tracks quickly

D. ▢ Honk your horn to alert the train of your presence


**14. What is the purpose of using proper ventilation when transporting hazardous materials?**

A. ▢ To prevent the buildup of harmful fumes or gases

B. ▢ To save on fuel consumption

C. ▢ To keep the cargo at an optimal temperature

D. ▢ To attract attention from other drivers on the road


**15. When transporting hazardous materials, it is important to:**

A. ▢ Have the appropriate fire extinguisher readily available

B. ▢ Drive at excessive speeds to minimize the time on the road

C. ▢ Ignore any weight restrictions on the vehicle

D. ▢ Overload the vehicle to maximize efficiency

# Correct answers for transportation of hazardous materials exam

1. **A.** Use caution and follow all regulations

2. **A.** To alert others of the potential hazards

3. **A.** Obtain the necessary permits and certifications

4. **A.** Stay clear of the area and notify the authorities

5. **A.** Follow established emergency procedures and seek assistance

6. **A.** The cargo being transported is highly combustible

7. **A.** Follow designated routes and avoid restricted areas

8. **A.** Stop in a safe location and inspect for leaks

9. **A.** Maintain control of the vehicle and safely pull over

10. **A.** Notify the authorities and follow emergency procedures

11. **A.** The cargo has the potential to cause chemical burns or damage

12 .**A.** Use proper restraints and containers as specified by regulations

13 . **A.** Stop, look, and listen for approaching trains

14. **A.** To prevent the buildup of harmful fumes or gases

15. **A.** Have the appropriate fire extinguisher readily available

# Transportation of hazardous materials exam 2

**1. When transporting hazardous materials, it is important to:**

A. ▢ Use caution and follow all regulations

B. ▢ Speed up to reach your destination faster

C. ▢ Ignore any weight restrictions

D. ▢ Keep the hazardous materials visible to other drivers


**2. What is the purpose of placards on vehicles transporting hazardous materials?**

A. ▢ To warn others of the potential hazards

B. ▢ To indicate the vehicle's weight capacity

C. ▢ To advertise the company's brand

D. ▢ To provide directions to the driver


**3. What should you do if you witness a hazardous materials spill on the road?**

A. ▢ Stay clear of the area and contact emergency services

B. ▢ Approach the spill to investigate the nature of the materials

C. ▢ Attempt to clean up the spill by yourself

D. ▢ Continue driving without taking any action


**4. How should you handle a vehicle breakdown when transporting hazardous materials?**

A. ▢ Follow proper procedures for securing and notifying authorities

B. ▢ Abandon the vehicle and leave the scene immediately

C. ▢ Transfer the hazardous materials to another vehicle on your own

D. ▢ Ignore the breakdown and continue driving

**5. What does the "Flammable" placard indicate on a vehicle transporting hazardous materials?**

A. ▢ The cargo being transported is highly flammable

B. ▢ The vehicle is carrying radioactive materials

C. ▢ The driver is transporting corrosive cleaning supplies

D. ▢ The cargo is safe and non-hazardous

**6. How should you secure hazardous materials in your vehicle?**

A. ▢ Use proper restraints and containers as specified by regulations

B. ▢ Place the materials loosely in the back of the vehicle

C. ▢ Ignore securing the materials to save time

D. ▢ Stack the materials as high as possible to maximize space

**7. What should you do if you encounter a railroad crossing while transporting hazardous materials?**

A. ▢ Stop, look, and listen for approaching trains

B. ▢ Ignore the crossing and proceed without caution

C. ▢ Increase your speed to cross the tracks quickly

D. ▢ Honk your horn to alert the train of your presence

**8. What is the purpose of using proper ventilation when transporting hazardous materials?**

A. ▢ To prevent the buildup of harmful fumes or gases

B. ▢ To save on fuel consumption

C. ▢ To keep the cargo at an optimal temperature

D. ▢ To attract attention from other drivers on the road

**9. When transporting hazardous materials, it is important to:**

A. ○ Have the appropriate fire extinguisher readily available

B. ○ Drive at excessive speeds to minimize the time on the road

C. ○ Ignore any weight restrictions on the vehicle

 D. ○ Overload the vehicle to maximize efficiency

**10. What is the purpose of a shipping paper when transporting hazardous materials?**

A. ○ To provide important information about the materials being transported

B. ○ To use as a source of entertainment during long trips

C. ○ To wrap the hazardous materials for extra protection

D. ○ To document any damages or spills during transportation

**11. When transporting hazardous materials, it is important to:**

A. ○ Keep a safe distance from other vehicles

B. ○ Tailgate other vehicles for increased visibility

C. ○ Drive in the center lane for better control

D. ○ Drive at high speeds to minimize the time on the road

**12. How should you respond if you suspect a leak or damage to a hazardous materials container?**

A. ○ Follow the proper procedures for reporting and addressing the situation

B. ○ Ignore the issue and continue driving to your destination

C. ○ Attempt to fix the container yourself

D. ○ Dispose of the container in a nearby trash bin

**13. What should you do if you encounter a hazardous materials emergency while driving?**

A. ▢ Safely pull over and contact emergency services

B. ▢ Drive faster to escape the area quickly

C. ▢ Take photos or videos of the emergency for documentation

D. ▢ Change your route to avoid the incident

**14. What does the "Corrosive" placard indicate on a vehicle transporting hazardous materials?**

A. ▢ The cargo being transported can cause damage upon contact

B. ▢ The vehicle is carrying radioactive materials

C. ▢ The driver is transporting flammable substances

D. ▢ The cargo is safe and non-hazardous

**15. When transporting hazardous materials, it is important to:**

A. ▢ Follow the designated routes and avoid restricted areas

B. ▢ Drive in any lane that is convenient for you

C. ▢ Ignore any weight restrictions on the vehicle

D. ▢ Exceed the speed limit to complete the trip faster

# Correct answers for transportation of hazardous materials exam 2

1.  **A.** Use caution and follow all regulations (To use caution and follow all regulations)

2.  **A.** To warn others of the potential hazards (To alert others of the potential hazards)

3.  **A.** Stay clear of the area and contact emergency services (Stay clear of the area and contact emergency services)

4.  **A.** Follow proper procedures for securing and notifying authorities (Follow proper procedures for securing and notifying authorities)

5.  **A.** The cargo being transported is highly flammable (The cargo being transported is highly flammable)

6.  **A.** Use proper restraints and containers as specified by regulations (Use proper restraints and containers as specified by regulations)

7.  **A.** Stop, look, and listen for approaching trains (Stop, look, and listen for approaching trains)

8.  **A.** To prevent the buildup of harmful fumes or gases (To prevent the buildup of harmful fumes or gases)

9.  **A.** Have the appropriate fire extinguisher readily available (Have the appropriate fire extinguisher readily available)

10. **A.** To provide important information about the materials being transported (To provide important information about the materials being transported)

11. **A.** Keep a safe distance from other vehicles (Keep a safe distance from other vehicles)

12. **A.** Follow the proper procedures for reporting and addressing the situation (Follow the proper procedures for reporting and addressing the situation)

13. **A.** Safely pull over and contact emergency services (Safely pull over and contact emergency services)

14. **A.** The cargo being transported can cause damage upon contact (The cargo being transported can cause damage upon contact)

15. **A.** Follow the designated routes and avoid restricted areas (Follow the designated routes and avoid restricted areas)

# Transportation of hazardous materials exam 3

**1. What should you do if you encounter a vehicle carrying hazardous materials that is on fire?**

A. ▢ Keep a safe distance and call emergency services immediately

B. ▢ Drive closer to provide assistance in extinguishing the fire

C. ▢ Pass the vehicle quickly to avoid exposure to the fire

D. ▢ Follow the vehicle closely to monitor the situation

**2. What does a "Flammable Gas" placard on a vehicle transporting hazardous materials indicate?**

A. ▢ The driver is transporting radioactive materials

B. ▢ The cargo being transported is a flammable gas

C. ▢ The vehicle is carrying explosive substances

D. ▢ The vehicle is well-maintained and in good working condition

**3. What should you do if you witness a hazardous materials spill on the road?**

A. ▢ Immediately contact emergency services and follow their instructions

B. ▢ Continue driving, as it is not your responsibility

C. ▢ Speed up to pass the area quickly

D. ▢ Inform other drivers to take a different route

**4. Why is it important to properly label packages containing hazardous materials?**

A. ▢ To meet legal requirements for shipping

B. ▢ To confuse potential thieves

C. ▢ To avoid any labeling altogether

D. ▢ To provide a detailed description of the contents being transported

**5. What should you do if you suspect a hazardous materials leak from another vehicle?**

A. ▢ Keep a safe distance and report the incident to authorities

B. ▢ Speed up and pass the vehicle quickly to avoid exposure

C. ▢ Ignore the situation and continue driving

D. ▢ Follow the vehicle closely to monitor the leak

**6. What is an important safety practice when transporting hazardous materials?**

A. ▢ Stay alert and focused on the road

B. ▢ Distract yourself with music or phone calls

C. ▢ Drive at excessive speeds to reach the destination quickly

D. ▢ Ignore any signs or warnings along the route

**7. What should you do if you discover a hazardous materials leak in your vehicle?**

A. ▢ Safely pull over and assess the situation

B. ▢ Continue driving and hope the leak stops on its own

C. ▢ Open the windows to ventilate the vehicle

D. ▢ Notify the nearest gas station

**8. What does an "Oxidizing Material" placard on a vehicle transporting hazardous materials indicate?**

A. ▢ The cargo being transported can cause or enhance combustion

B. ▢ The vehicle is carrying radioactive materials

C. ▢ The driver is transporting corrosive substances

D. ▢ The cargo is safe and non-reactive

**9. Why is it important for drivers transporting hazardous materials to be aware of the emergency response guidebook?**

A. ▢ It provides essential information on how to handle different hazardous materials

B. ▢ It is required by law to carry the guidebook at all times

C. ▢ It helps drivers navigate unfamiliar routes

D. ▢ It contains important traffic laws and regulations

**10. When transporting hazardous materials, what should you do to ensure compliance with regulations?**

A. ▢ Follow the specific regulations for each type of hazardous material

B. ▢ Ignore any regulations that seem unnecessary

C. ▢ Transport smaller quantities of hazardous materials to avoid compliance

D. ▢ Delegate compliance responsibilities to someone else

**11. What should you do if you come across a vehicle transporting radioactive materials that has been involved in an accident?**

A. ▢ Keep a safe distance and call emergency services immediately

B. ▢ Approach the vehicle to offer assistance

C. ▢ Drive alongside the vehicle to document the accident

D. ▢ Ignore the situation and continue driving

**12. What does a "Corrosive" placard on a vehicle transporting hazardous materials indicate?**

A. ▢ The cargo being transported is corrosive

B. ▢ The vehicle is carrying flammable substances

C. ▢ The driver is transporting radioactive materials

D. ▢ The cargo is safe and non-reactive

**13. How should hazardous materials packages be marked?**

A. ▢ Clearly mark them with the appropriate hazard symbols and information

B. ▢ Leave them unmarked to avoid drawing attention

C. ▢ Mark them with misleading information to confuse potential thieves

D. ▢ Use generic labels for all packages, regardless of their contents

**14. What should you do if you encounter a vehicle transporting hazardous materials involved in a collision?**

A. ▢ Keep a safe distance and report the incident to authorities

B. ▢ Drive closer to assess the damage

C. ▢ Continue driving without stopping

D. ▢ Approach the vehicle to offer assistance

**15. What should you do if you are asked to transport hazardous materials but feel uncomfortable doing so?**

A. ▢ Decline the transportation request and suggest an alternative method

B. ▢ Accept the request without any hesitation

C. ▢ Transport the materials at a higher cost

D. ▢ Transfer the responsibility to another driver

# Correct answers for transportation of hazardous materials exam 3

1. **A.** Keep a safe distance and call emergency services immediately

2. **B.** The cargo being transported is a flammable gas

3. **A.** Immediately contact emergency services and follow their instructions

4. **A.** To meet legal requirements for shipping

5. **A.** Keep a safe distance and report the incident to authorities

6. **A** .Stay alert and focused on the road

7. **A.** Safely pull over and assess the situation

8. **A.** The cargo being transported can cause or enhance combustion

9. **A.** It provides essential information on how to handle different hazardous materials

10. **A.** Follow the specific regulations for each type of hazardous material

11. **A.** Keep a safe distance and call emergency services immediately

12. **A.** The cargo being transported is corrosive

13. **A.** Clearly mark them with the appropriate hazard symbols and information

14. **A.** Keep a safe distance and report the incident to authorities

15. **A.** Decline the transportation request and suggest an alternative method

# Transportation of hazardous materials exam 4

**1. What should you do if you notice a leak in a container carrying hazardous materials?**

A. ▢ Safely move the container to an open area

B. ▢ Ignore the leak and continue transporting the container

C. ▢ Seal the leak with duct tape to prevent further leakage

D. ▢ Contact the appropriate authorities and follow their instructions


**2. What does a "Radioactive" placard on a vehicle transporting hazardous materials indicate?**

A. ▢ The vehicle is carrying flammable substances

B. ▢ The cargo being transported is radioactive materials

C. ▢ The driver is transporting corrosive substances

D. ▢ The cargo is safe and non-reactive


**3. How should hazardous materials be stored during transportation?**

A. ▢ Securely and separate from incompatible materials

B. ▢ Loosely to allow for easy access during inspections

C. ▢ Packed tightly to maximize space in the vehicle

D. ▢ Mixed with other materials to reduce the risk of spills


**4. What should you do if you come across an overturned vehicle carrying hazardous materials?**

A. ▢ Keep a safe distance and contact emergency services immediately

B. ▢ Approach the vehicle to assess the damage

C. ▢ Drive closer to document the incident

D. ▢ Ignore the situation and continue driving

**5. Why is it important to have proper ventilation when transporting certain hazardous materials?**

A. ▢ To prevent the accumulation of flammable or toxic vapors

B. ▢ To keep the cargo cool during transportation

C. ▢ To avoid excessive weight in the vehicle

D. ▢ To save fuel and reduce transportation costs

**6. What should you do if you suspect a hazardous materials package is damaged?**

A. ▢ Handle the package with caution and report it immediately

B. ▢ Open the package to inspect its contents

C. ▢ Continue transporting the package without any concern

D. ▢ Place the package in a separate compartment to avoid contact with other materials

**7. What does a "Dangerous When Wet" placard on a vehicle transporting hazardous materials indicate?**

A. ▢ The cargo being transported can react violently with water

B. ▢ The vehicle is carrying radioactive materials

C. ▢ The driver is transporting flammable substances

D. ▢ The cargo is safe and non-reactive

**8. How often should drivers transporting hazardous materials inspect their vehicles?**

A. ▢ Before each trip and at regular intervals during the trip

B. ▢ Once a week, regardless of the number of trips made

C. ▢ Only when there is a visible issue with the vehicle

D. ▢ At the end of each trip, before starting a new one

**9. What should you do if you suspect a cargo of hazardous materials is leaking from your vehicle?**

A. ▢ Pull over in a safe location and address the leak immediately

B. ▢ Speed up to reach your destination quickly and dispose of the cargo

C. ▢ Ignore the leak and continue driving as usual

D. ▢ Transfer the cargo to another vehicle and continue driving

**10. What does a "Non-Flammable Gas" placard on a vehicle transporting hazardous materials indicate?**

A. ▢ The cargo being transported is a non-flammable gas

B. ▢ The vehicle is carrying explosive substances

C. ▢ The driver is transporting corrosive substances

D. ▢ The cargo is safe and non-reactive

**11. How should you handle damaged or leaking packages of hazardous materials during transportation?**

A. ▢ Isolate the package and contact the appropriate authorities

B. ▢ Open the package to inspect its contents

C. ▢ Place the package in a regular trash container

D. ▢ Continue transporting the package without any concern

**12. What should you do if you encounter a vehicle transporting hazardous materials displaying a "Fire" placard?**

A. ▢ Keep a safe distance and call emergency services immediately

B. ▢ Drive alongside the vehicle to document the situation

C. ▢ Approach the vehicle to offer assistance

D. ▢ Ignore the situation and continue driving

**13. How should hazardous materials be loaded and unloaded from a vehicle?**

A. ▢ Follow the specific procedures and guidelines provided for each material

B. ▢ Load and unload all materials in a haphazard manner

C. ▢ Ask bystanders to assist in the loading and unloading process

D. ▢ Handle all materials using bare hands and without any protective equipment

**14. What should you do if you suspect a hazardous materials container is leaking while in transit?**

A. ▢ Stop the vehicle in a safe location and report the incident immediately

B. ▢ Continue driving until you reach your destination and then inspect the container

C. ▢ Ignore the leak and hope it will stop on its own

D. ▢ Transfer the leaking materials to a different container

**15. Why is it important to properly secure hazardous materials during transportation?**

A. ▢ To prevent the materials from shifting or falling during transit

B. ▢ To reduce the weight of the vehicle

C. ▢ To make it easier to access the materials during inspections

D. ▢ To save time and avoid delays in delivery

# Correct answers for transportation of hazardous materials exam 4

**1. A** (Safely move the container to an open area)

**2. B** (The cargo being transported is radioactive materials)

**3. A** (Securely and separate from incompatible materials)

**4. A** (Keep a safe distance and contact emergency services immediately)

**5. A** (To prevent the accumulation of flammable or toxic vapors)

**6. A** (Handle the package with caution and report it immediately)

**7. A** (The cargo being transported can react violently with water)

**8. A** (Before each trip and at regular intervals during the trip)

**9. A** (Pull over in a safe location and address the leak immediately)

**10. A** (The cargo being transported is a non-flammable gas)

**11. A** (Isolate the package and contact the appropriate authorities)

**12. A** (Keep a safe distance and call emergency services immediately)

**13. A** (Follow the specific procedures and guidelines provided for each material)

**14. A** (Stop the vehicle in a safe location and report the incident immediately)

**15. A** (To prevent the materials from shifting or falling during transit)

# Transportation of hazardous materials exam 5

1.  What does the "Flammable Solid" placard on a vehicle carrying hazardous materials indicate?

A. ▢ The cargo being transported is highly explosive

B. ▢ The vehicle is carrying radioactive materials

C. ▢ The driver is transporting flammable solids

D. ▢ The cargo is safe and non-reactive

2.  What should you do if you suspect a chemical spill has occurred during the transportation of hazardous materials?

A. ▢ Immediately notify emergency services and follow their instructions

B. ▢ Continue driving and monitor the situation closely

C. ▢ Wait until you reach your destination before addressing the spill

D. ▢ Ignore the spill if it appears minor

3. How should hazardous materials be labeled for transportation?

A. ▢ Clearly and prominently, in accordance with regulatory requirements

B. ▢ With minimal labeling to avoid drawing attention

C. ▢ Only if the materials are considered extremely hazardous

D. ▢ Labeled with generic terms to prevent identification

**4. What is the purpose of a Material Safety Data Sheet (MSDS) for hazardous materials?**

A. ▢ To provide information about the properties and hazards of the materials

B. ▢ To list the various routes for transporting hazardous materials

C. ▢ To identify the potential cost savings associated with the materials

D. ▢ To promote the use of hazardous materials in everyday life

**5. When transporting hazardous materials, what should you do if you are involved in a traffic collision?**

A. ▢ Notify emergency services and inform them about the materials being transported

B. ▢ Keep the information about the hazardous materials to yourself

C. ▢ Attempt to clean up any spilled materials before authorities arrive

D. ▢ Leave the scene immediately and report the incident later

**6. What does the "Corrosive" placard on a vehicle transporting hazardous materials indicate?**

A. ▢ The vehicle is carrying radioactive materials

B. ▢ The driver is transporting flammable substances

C. ▢ The cargo being transported can cause corrosion or burns

D. ▢ The cargo is safe and non-reactive

**7. What should you do if you encounter a vehicle transporting hazardous materials that is emitting strong odors?**

A. ▢ Keep a safe distance and report the incident to authorities

B. ▢ Drive alongside the vehicle to assess the source of the odor

C. ▢ Ignore the situation and continue driving

D. ▢ Open your windows to ventilate your own vehicle

**8. How should you handle damaged containers of hazardous materials during transportation?**

A. ▢ Isolate the damaged containers and contact the appropriate authorities

B. ▢ Discard the damaged containers at the nearest waste disposal site

C. ▢ Transfer the contents of the damaged containers to new containers

D. ▢ Ignore the damage and continue transporting the containers

**9. What should you do if you suspect a cargo of hazardous materials is reacting with its packaging?**

A. ▢ Pull over in a safe location and contact emergency services

B. ▢ Continue transporting the cargo and monitor the situation

C. ▢ Open the packaging to investigate the reaction

D. ▢ Dispose of the cargo immediately

**10. What does the "Toxic" placard on a vehicle transporting hazardous materials indicate?**

A. ▢ The cargo being transported is highly flammable

B. ▢ The driver is transporting corrosive substances

C. ▢ The cargo can cause severe illness or death

D. ▢ The cargo poses no threat to human health

**11. How often should you inspect your vehicle when transporting hazardous materials?**

A. ▢ Before each trip and at regular intervals during the trip

B. ▢ Only when you suspect a problem with the cargo

C. ▢ Once a month, regardless of the distance traveled

D. ▢ Inspections are not necessary for vehicles transporting hazardous materials

**12. What should you do if you notice a hazardous materials container leaking while in transit?**

A. ▢ Stop the vehicle in a safe location and report the incident immediately

B. ▢ Continue driving and monitor the leak closely

C. ▢ Transfer the leaking materials to a different container

D. ▢ Ignore the leak and hope it stops on its own

**13. Why is it important to separate incompatible hazardous materials during transportation?**

A. ▢ To prevent the materials from reacting and causing dangerous situations

B. ▢ To save space and increase the cargo capacity of the vehicle

C. ▢ To reduce the weight of the vehicle and improve fuel efficiency

D. ▢ Separation is not necessary for transporting hazardous materials

**14. What is the primary reason for securing hazardous materials properly during transportation?**

A. ▢ To prevent the materials from shifting or falling during transit

B. ▢ To minimize the risk of theft or unauthorized access to the materials

C. ▢ To comply with weight regulations imposed on commercial vehicles

D. ▢ Proper securing is not necessary for transporting hazardous materials

**15. How should you handle a package labeled as "Radioactive" during transportation?**

A. ▢ Handle the package with caution and report it immediately

B. ▢ Place the package in a regular trash container

C. ▢ Ignore the label and handle the package as any other package

D. ▢ Open the package to inspect its contents

# Correct answers for transportation of hazardous materials exam 5

**1. C** (The driver is transporting flammable solids)

**2. A** (Immediately notify emergency services and follow their instructions)

**3. A** (Clearly and prominently, in accordance with regulatory requirements)

**4. A** (To provide information about the properties and hazards of the materials)

**5. A** (Notify emergency services and inform them about the materials being transported)

**6. C** (The cargo being transported can cause corrosion or burns)

**7. A** (Keep a safe distance and report the incident to authorities)

**8. A** (Isolate the damaged containers and contact the appropriate authorities)

**9. A** (Pull over in a safe location and contact emergency services)

**10. C** (The cargo can cause severe illness or death)

**11. A** (Before each trip and at regular intervals during the trip)

**12. A** (Stop the vehicle in a safe location and report the incident immediately)

**13. A** (To prevent the materials from reacting and causing dangerous situations)

**14. A** (To prevent the materials from shifting or falling during transit)

**15. A** (Handle the package with caution and report it immediately)

# Vehicle registration and insurance

Welcome to Chapter 7 of the Minnesota DMV Exam Workbook, where we explore the essential topics of vehicle registration and insurance. In this chapter, we will delve into the requirements, processes, and importance of vehicle registration and insurance in the state of Minnesota. Understanding the legal obligations and financial protections associated with vehicle ownership is crucial for responsible and compliant driving.

## The Importance of Vehicle Registration

Vehicle registration is a legal requirement that ensures accountability, traceability, and the proper identification of vehicles on Minnesota's roads. This section will emphasize the significance of vehicle registration, highlighting the role it plays in maintaining accurate records, facilitating law enforcement, and protecting public safety. By registering your vehicle, you contribute to the overall integrity and efficiency of the state's transportation system.

## Vehicle Registration Process

This section will provide a comprehensive overview of the vehicle registration process in Minnesota. We will explore the necessary documentation, such as proof of ownership, title transfer, and vehicle identification number (VIN) verification. We will also discuss the fees associated with registration and the importance of renewing registration on time to avoid penalties.

## License Plates and Registration Stickers

License plates and registration stickers serve as visual identifiers for registered vehicles. This section will cover the design, placement, and requirements for license plates and registration stickers in Minnesota. We will discuss the significance of properly displaying these identifiers and the consequences of tampering or unauthorized use.

## Vehicle Insurance Requirements

Vehicle insurance is a crucial aspect of responsible vehicle ownership, providing financial protection in the event of accidents, damage, or injuries. This section will explore the insurance requirements for vehicle owners in Minnesota. We will discuss the types of coverage available, such as liability, comprehensive, and collision, and the minimum coverage limits mandated by law. Understanding insurance requirements helps ensure financial security and compliance with state regulations.

## Proof of Insurance

This section will outline the importance of carrying proof of insurance while operating a vehicle in Minnesota. We will explore the acceptable forms of proof, such as insurance cards, digital copies, or electronic verification. Additionally, we will discuss the consequences of failing to provide proof of insurance when requested by law enforcement or during vehicle registration.

## Insurance Claims and Reporting Accidents

In the unfortunate event of an accident, understanding the insurance claims process is crucial. This section will provide an overview of the steps to take when filing an insurance claim and reporting accidents to your insurance company. We will discuss the importance of timely reporting, gathering evidence, and cooperating with insurance adjusters to expedite the claims process.

## Uninsured and Underinsured Motorist Coverage

Uninsured and underinsured motorist coverage is an additional layer of protection for vehicle owners in Minnesota. This section will explain the importance of this coverage, especially in situations where the at-fault party lacks sufficient insurance coverage. We will explore the benefits of uninsured and underinsured motorist coverage and the options available to vehicle owners in Minnesota.

## Vehicle Registration and Insurance Renewal

Renewal of vehicle registration and insurance policies is essential for maintaining compliance and continuous coverage. This section will discuss the renewal processes for both vehicle registration and insurance in Minnesota. We will emphasize the importance of timely renewals to avoid penalties, gaps in coverage, and potential legal consequences.

## Vehicle Registration and Insurance Fraud

Vehicle registration and insurance fraud pose significant risks to individuals, the insurance industry, and society as a whole. This section will explore common types of fraud, such as providing false information, staged accidents, or insurance scams. We will highlight the consequences of engaging in fraudulent activities and the importance of reporting any suspicions or incidents of fraud.

## Conclusion

By understanding the requirements and processes associated with vehicle registration and insurance, you are taking proactive steps towards responsible vehicle ownership and compliance with Minnesota's laws. Throughout this chapter, we will delve deeper into the specific aspects of vehicle registration and insurance, providing you with the knowledge and resources necessary to navigate the registration process, select appropriate insurance coverage, and ensure financial protection. So, let's embark on this journey of legal compliance and financial security, fostering responsible vehicle ownership in the Land of 10,000 Lakes.

For training purposes, you can mark the ▢ symbol next to what you think is the correct answer: Once you have chosen the correct answer, use a pencil or pen to mark the ▢ symbol next to that answer.

So let's get started!

# Vehicle registration and insurance exam

**1. How often must you renew your vehicle registration in Minnesota?**

A. ▢ Every 2 years

B. ▢ Every 3 years

C. ▢ Every 4 years

D. ▢ Every 5 years

**2. What documents are typically required for vehicle registration in Minnesota?**

A. ▢ Proof of insurance, vehicle title, and driver's license

B. ▢ Vehicle inspection report and social security card

C. ▢ Proof of address and birth certificate

D. ▢ None, vehicle registration is automatic in Minnesota

**3. What should you do if you change your address while residing in Minnesota?**

A. ▢ Notify the Minnesota MVC within one week

B. ▢ Update your address on your vehicle registration only

C. ▢ Wait until your next vehicle registration renewal to update your address

D. ▢ It is not necessary to update your address with the MVC

**4. In Minnesota, all registered vehicles must have what minimum level of insurance coverage?**

A. ▢ Liability insurance

B. ▢ Comprehensive insurance

C. ▢ Collision insurance

D. ▢ No insurance is required in Minnesota

**5. What is the purpose of having insurance coverage for your vehicle?**

A. ▢ To protect yourself financially in case of an accident

B. ▢ To avoid vehicle inspections by law enforcement

C. ▢ To provide additional security against theft

D. ▢ Insurance coverage is not necessary in Minnesota


**6. What should you do if you sell or transfer ownership of your vehicle in Minnesota?**

A. ▢ Notify the Minnesota MVC within 10 days

B. ▢ Cancel your insurance policy immediately

C. ▢ Wait for the new owner to update the registration

D. ▢ There is no need to inform the MVC about the sale or transfer


**7. What is the purpose of vehicle registration in Minnesota?**

A. ▢ To establish ownership and legal operation of the vehicle

B. ▢ To determine the vehicle's market value for resale purposes

C. ▢ To track the vehicle's mileage and fuel consumption

D. ▢ Vehicle registration is not required in Minnesota


**8. What should you do if your vehicle registration card is lost or stolen?**

A. ▢ Apply for a duplicate registration card from the Minnesota MVC

B. ▢ Continue driving without a registration card

C. ▢ Register the vehicle again as if it were new

D. ▢ Ignore the loss and hope it turns up eventually

**9. When is it necessary to provide proof of insurance for your vehicle in Minnesota?**

A. ▢ During vehicle registration, renewal, and upon request by law enforcement

B. ▢ Only when involved in a traffic accident

C. ▢ Once every five years, regardless of other circumstances

D. ▢ Proof of insurance is not required in Minnesota

**10. What should you do if your insurance policy is canceled or expires while your vehicle is registered in Minnesota?**

A. ▢ Obtain a new insurance policy and provide proof to the MVC

B. ▢ Continue driving without insurance coverage

C. ▢ Wait until your next vehicle registration renewal to update your insurance information

D. ▢ It is not necessary to have continuous insurance coverage in Minnesota

**11. In Minnesota, what is the consequence for operating a vehicle without valid registration?**

A. ▢ Fines, vehicle impoundment, and suspension of driving privileges

B. ▢ Verbal warning from law enforcement

C. ▢ Reduced vehicle inspection frequency

D. ▢ No consequences, as vehicle registration is not enforced

**12. What is the purpose of vehicle insurance in Minnesota?**

A. ▢ To provide financial protection in case of accidents or damage

B. ▢ To increase the resale value of the vehicle

C. ▢ To cover routine maintenance and repairs

D. ▢ Vehicle insurance is not required in Minnesota

**13. What is the penalty for driving without valid insurance in Minnesota?**

A. ▢ Fines, suspension of driving privileges, and vehicle impoundment

B. ▢ Verbal warning from law enforcement

C. ▢ Reduction in vehicle registration fees

D. ▢ No penalty, as insurance is not required in Minnesota

**14. When should you notify your insurance company about changes in your vehicle's usage, such as using it for commercial purposes?**

A. ▢ Immediately, to ensure proper coverage

B. ▢ Only if specifically requested by the insurance company

C. ▢ Once a year, during vehicle inspection

D. ▢ It is not necessary to notify the insurance company about changes in usage

**15. What is the purpose of having a valid vehicle registration sticker displayed on your license plate?**

A. ▢ To show that your vehicle's registration is current

B. ▢ To indicate that your vehicle has passed a recent inspection

C. ▢ To increase the vehicle's visibility at night

D. ▢ Vehicle registration stickers are not required in Minnesota

# Correct answers for vehicle registration and insurance exam

**1. C** (Every 4 years)

**2. A** (Proof of insurance, vehicle title, and driver's license)

**3. A** (Notify the Minnesota MVC within one week)

**4. A** (Liability insurance)

**5. A** (To protect yourself financially in case of an accident)

**6. A** (Notify the Minnesota MVC within 10 days)

**7. A** (To establish ownership and legal operation of the vehicle)

**8. A** (Apply for a duplicate registration card from the Minnesota MVC)

**9. A** (During vehicle registration, renewal, and upon request by law enforcement)

**10. A** (Obtain a new insurance policy and provide proof to the MVC)

**11. A** (Fines, vehicle impoundment, and suspension of driving privileges)

**12. A** (To provide financial protection in case of accidents or damage)

**13. A** (Fines, suspension of driving privileges, and vehicle impoundment)

**14. A** (Immediately, to ensure proper coverage)

**15. A** (To show that your vehicle's registration is current)

# Vehicle registration and insurance exam 2

**1. How soon must you notify your insurance company after purchasing a new vehicle in Minnesota?**

A. ▢ Within 24 hours

B. ▢ Within 48 hours

C. ▢ Within 72 hours

D. ▢ Within 7 days

**2. What is the purpose of having uninsured motorist coverage on your insurance policy?**

A. ▢ To protect you financially if you are involved in an accident with an uninsured driver

B. ▢ To provide coverage for damage caused by natural disasters

C. ▢ To cover the cost of routine vehicle maintenance

D. ▢ Uninsured motorist coverage is not required in Minnesota

**3. In Minnesota, if your vehicle is leased or financed, who typically holds the vehicle's title?**

A. ▢ The leasing or financing company

B. ▢ The vehicle manufacturer

C. ▢ The Minnesota MVC

D. ▢ The vehicle owner

**4. What is the penalty for driving without valid insurance in Minnesota?**

A. ▢ Fines, suspension of driving privileges, and vehicle impoundment

B. ▢ Verbal warning from law enforcement

C. ▢ Reduction in vehicle registration fees

D. ▢ No penalty, as insurance is not required in Minnesota

**5. What should you do if your insurance policy is canceled or expires while your vehicle is registered in Minnesota?**

A. ▢ Obtain a new insurance policy and provide proof to the MVC

B. ▢ Continue driving without insurance coverage

C. ▢ Wait until your next vehicle registration renewal to update your insurance information

D. ▢ It is not necessary to have continuous insurance coverage in Minnesota

**6. What is the purpose of having personal injury protection (PIP) coverage on your insurance policy in Minnesota?**

A. ▢ To cover medical expenses for injuries sustained in an accident

B. ▢  To protect against damage caused by theft or vandalism

C. ▢ To provide coverage for rental vehicles

D. ▢ Personal injury protection coverage is not required in Minnesota

**7. What is the grace period for renewing your vehicle registration in Minnesota?**

A. ▢ 1 month

B. ▢ 2 months

C. ▢ 3 months

D. ▢ There is no grace period

**8. What should you do if you receive a notice of insurance lapse from the Minnesota MVC?**

A. ▢ Provide proof of insurance coverage immediately

B. ▢ Ignore the notice, as it may be an error

C. ▢ Contact the MVC to contest the notice

D. ▢ Cancel your vehicle registration

**9. In Minnesota, what is the purpose of having a valid insurance identification card?**

A. ▢ To provide proof of insurance coverage when requested by law enforcement or during vehicle inspections

B. ▢ To track your vehicle's mileage and fuel consumption

C. ▢ To indicate the expiration date of your vehicle registration

D. ▢ Insurance identification cards are not required in Minnesota

**10. What should you do if you sell or transfer ownership of your vehicle in Minnesota?**

A. ▢ Notify the Minnesota MVC within 10 days

B. ▢ Cancel your insurance policy immediately

C. ▢ Wait for the new owner to update the registration

D. ▢ There is no need to inform the MVC about the sale or transfer

**11. What is the purpose of having comprehensive coverage on your insurance policy in Minnesota?**

A. ▢ To cover damage to your vehicle caused by non-collision events, such as theft, vandalism, or natural disasters

B. ▢ To provide coverage for injuries sustained in an accident

C. ▢ To cover the cost of routine vehicle maintenance

D. ▢ Comprehensive coverage is not required in Minnesota

**12. How often must you renew your vehicle registration in Minnesota?**

A. ○ Annually

B. ○ Biennially (every 2 years)

C. ○ Triennially (every 3 years)

D. ○ Every 4 years

**13. What documents are required to register a vehicle in Minnesota?**

A. ○ Proof of insurance, vehicle title, and driver's license

B. ○ Vehicle inspection report, vehicle history report, and proof of address

C. ○ Social Security card, birth certificate, and passport

D. ○ Vehicle registration is not required in Minnesota

**14. What is the procedure for updating your insurance information with the Minnesota MVC?**

A. ○ Notify the Minnesota MVC within one week of any changes

B. ○ Send a copy of your updated insurance policy to the MVC annually

C. ○ Update your insurance information during your next vehicle inspection

D. ○ It is not necessary to update your insurance information with the MVC

**15. What is the purpose of vehicle registration in Minnesota?**

A. ○ To establish ownership and legal operation of the vehicle

B. ○ To indicate that your vehicle has passed a recent inspection

C. ○ To increase the vehicle's visibility at night

D. ○ Vehicle registration is not required in Minnesota

# Correct answers for vehicle registration and insurance exam 2

**1. D** (Within 7 days)

**2. A** (To protect you financially if you are involved in an accident with an uninsured driver)

**3. A** (The leasing or financing company)

**4. A** (Fines, suspension of driving privileges, and vehicle impoundment)

**5. A** (Obtain a new insurance policy and provide proof to the MVC)

**6. A** (To cover medical expenses for injuries sustained in an accident)

**7. D** (There is no grace period)

**8. A** (Provide proof of insurance coverage immediately)

**9. A** (To provide proof of insurance coverage when requested by law enforcement or during vehicle inspections)

**10. A** (Notify the Minnesota MVC within 10 days)

**11. A** (To cover damage to your vehicle caused by non-collision events, such as theft, vandalism, or natural disasters)

**12. A** (Annually)

**13. A** (Proof of insurance, vehicle title, and driver's license)

**14. A** (Notify the Minnesota MVC within one week of any changes)

**15. A** (To establish ownership and legal operation of the vehicle)

# Vehicle registration and insurance exam 3

**1. What is the minimum liability insurance coverage required for private passenger vehicles in Minnesota?**

A. ▢ $10,000 per person, $30,000 per accident

B. ▢ $15,000 per person, $30,000 per accident

C. ▢ $25,000 per person, $50,000 per accident

D. ▢ $50,000 per person, $100,000 per accident

**2. How long do you have to report a change of address for your vehicle registration in Minnesota?**

A. ▢ Within 30 days

B. ▢ Within 60 days

C. ▢ Within 90 days

D. ▢ Within 120 days

**3. What should you do if your vehicle is involved in an accident and you have insurance?**

A. ▢ Report the accident to your insurance company

B. ▢ Ignore the accident if there are no injuries

C. ▢ Exchange information with the other driver and leave the scene

D. ▢ Wait for law enforcement to contact you

**4. Which of the following documents is required to prove your identity when registering a vehicle in Minnesota?**

A. ▢ Social Security card

B. ▢ Birth certificate

C. ▢ Passport

D. ▢ Driver's license

**5. What is the purpose of having underinsured motorist coverage on your insurance policy?**

A. ▢ To protect you financially if you are involved in an accident with a driver who has insufficient insurance coverage

B. ▢ To cover the cost of vehicle repairs due to mechanical failure

C. ▢ To provide coverage for rental vehicles

D. ▢ Underinsured motorist coverage is not required in Minnesota

**6. How often must you update your vehicle insurance information with the Minnesota MVC?**

A. ▢ Annually

B. ▢ Biennially (every 2 years)

C. ▢ Triennially (every 3 years)

D. ▢ Only when you change insurance providers

**7. What is the penalty for driving without valid vehicle registration in Minnesota?**

A. ▢ Fines, suspension of driving privileges, and possible vehicle impoundment

B. ▢ Verbal warning from law enforcement

C. ▢ Reduction in vehicle insurance premiums

D. ▢ No penalty, as vehicle registration is not required in Minnesota

**8. When must you obtain a temporary license plate for a newly purchased vehicle in Minnesota?**

A. ▢ Within 10 days of purchase

B. ▢ Within 20 days of purchase

C. ▢ Within 30 days of purchase

D. ▢ Temporary license plates are not required in Minnesota

**9. How long is a vehicle registration valid in Minnesota?**

A. ▢ 1 year

B. ▢ 2 years

C. ▢ 3 years

D. ▢ 4 years

**10. What should you do if you receive a notice of insurance cancellation from your insurance company?**

A. ▢ Obtain new insurance coverage and provide proof to the MVC

B. ▢ Ignore the notice and continue driving without insurance

C. ▢ Contact your insurance company to contest the cancellation

D. ▢ Cancel your vehicle registration immediately

**11. What is the purpose of having rental reimbursement coverage on your insurance policy?**

A. ▢ To cover the cost of a rental vehicle while your insured vehicle is being repaired after an accident

B. ▢ To provide coverage for rental vehicles during vacation trips

C. ▢ To reimburse you for fuel expenses during road trips

D. ▢ Rental reimbursement coverage is not available in Minnesota

**12. How can you provide proof of insurance coverage to the Minnesota MVC?**

A. ▢ By showing an insurance identification card provided by your insurance company

B. ▢ By presenting a copy of your insurance policy

C. ▢ By providing a letter from your insurance agent

D. ▢ Proof of insurance coverage is not required in Minnesota

**13. What is the penalty for driving without valid insurance in Minnesota?**

A. ▢ Fines, suspension of driving privileges, and possible vehicle impoundment

B. ▢ Verbal warning from law enforcement

C. ▢ Reduction in vehicle registration fees

D. ▢ No penalty, as insurance coverage is not required in Minnesota

**14. How long do you have to report a change of insurance provider to the Minnesota MVC?**

A. ▢ Within 10 days

B. ▢ Within 30 days

C. ▢ Within 60 days

D. ▢ No need to report a change of insurance provider to the MVC

**15. What is the purpose of having collision coverage on your insurance policy?**

A. ▢ To cover damage to your own vehicle caused by a collision with another vehicle or object

B. ▢ To provide coverage for medical expenses in case of an accident

C. ▢ To cover the cost of routine vehicle maintenance

D. ▢ Collision coverage is not required in Minnesota

# Correct answers for vehicle registration and insurance exam 3

**1. C** ($25,000 per person, $50,000 per accident)

**2. A** (Within 30 days)

**3. A** (Report the accident to your insurance company)

**4. D** (Driver's license)

**5. A** (To protect you financially if you are involved in an accident with a driver who has insufficient insurance coverage)

**6. A** (Annually)

**7. A** (Fines, suspension of driving privileges, and possible vehicle impoundment)

**8. A** (Within 10 days of purchase)

**9. A** (1 year)

**10. A** (Obtain new insurance coverage and provide proof to the MVC)

**11. A** (To cover the cost of a rental vehicle while your insured vehicle is being repaired after an accident)

**12. A** (By showing an insurance identification card provided by your insurance company)

**13. A** (Fines, suspension of driving privileges, and possible vehicle impoundment)

**14. B** (Within 30 days)

**15. A** (To cover damage to your own vehicle caused by a collision with another vehicle or object)

# Vehicle registration and insurance exam 4

1. What type of insurance coverage protects you against damage to your own vehicle in an accident?

A. ▢ Liability insurance

B. ▢ Comprehensive insurance

C. ▢ Personal injury protection

D. ▢ Uninsured motorist coverage

2. When should you notify your insurance company about modifications or changes made to your vehicle?

A. ▢ Within 10 days

B. ▢ Within 30 days

C. ▢ Within 60 days

D. ▢ No need to notify the insurance company

3. What is the purpose of personal injury protection (PIP) insurance in Minnesota?

A. ▢ To cover medical expenses for injuries sustained in a car accident

B. ▢ To provide coverage for vehicle repairs

C. ▢ To protect against theft or vandalism

D. ▢ Personal injury protection is not required in Minnesota

**4. What is the minimum amount of liability insurance coverage required for property damage in Minnesota?**

A. ▢ $5,000

B. ▢ $10,000

C. ▢ $15,000

D. ▢ $25,000

**5. What should you do if you receive a notice of insurance non-renewal from your insurance company?**

A. ▢ Seek coverage from a different insurance company

B. ▢ Continue driving without insurance

C. ▢ Contact the insurance company to discuss the non-renewal

D. ▢ Ignore the notice and hope for the best

**6. How often must you renew your vehicle registration in Minnesota?**

A. ▢ Annually

B. ▢ Biennially (every 2 years)

C. ▢ Triennially (every 3 years)

D. ▢ Only when you change vehicles

**7. What is the purpose of having comprehensive insurance coverage on your policy?**

A. ▢ To protect against damage to your vehicle from non-collision events

B. ▢ To cover medical expenses for injuries sustained in a car accident

C. ▢ To provide coverage for rental vehicles

D. ▢ Comprehensive insurance coverage is not required in Minnesota

**8. How long do you have to notify the Minnesota MVC about a change of insurance coverage?**

A. ▢ Within 5 days

B. ▢ Within 10 days

C. ▢ Within 30 days

D. ▢ No need to notify the MVC

**9. Which of the following is required when registering a leased vehicle in Minnesota?**

A. ▢ Proof of insurance coverage

B. ▢ Original vehicle title

C. ▢ Copy of the lease agreement

D. ▢ Vehicle bill of sale

**10. What is the penalty for driving without valid insurance in Minnesota?**

A. ▢ Fines, suspension of driving privileges, and possible vehicle impoundment

B. ▢ Verbal warning from law enforcement

C. ▢ Reduction in vehicle registration fees

D. ▢ No penalty, as insurance coverage is not required in Minnesota

**11. When should you notify your insurance company about a change of address?**

A. ▢ Within 10 days

B. ▢ Within 30 days

C. ▢ Within 60 days

D. ▢ No need to notify the insurance company

**12. What is the purpose of having uninsured motorist coverage on your insurance policy?**

A. ☐ To protect you financially if you are involved in an accident with an uninsured driver

B. ☐ To provide coverage for medical expenses in case of an accident

C. ☐ To cover the cost of vehicle repairs

D. ☐ Uninsured motorist coverage is not required in Minnesota

**13. How long do you have to report a change of insurance provider to the Minnesota MVC?**

A. ☐ Within 10 days

B. ☐ Within 30 days

C. ☐ Within 60 days

D. ☐ No need to report a change of insurance provider to the MVC

**14. What is the purpose of having collision coverage on your insurance policy?**

A. ☐ To cover damage to your own vehicle caused by a collision with another vehicle or object

B. ☐ To provide coverage for medical expenses in case of an accident

C. ☐ To cover the cost of routine vehicle maintenance

D. ☐ Collision coverage is not required in Minnesota

**15. What is the penalty for driving with an expired vehicle registration in Minnesota?**

A. ☐ Fines and possible suspension of driving privileges

B. ☐ Verbal warning from law enforcement

C. ☐ Reduction in vehicle insurance premiums

D. ☐ No penalty, as vehicle registration is not required in Minnesota

# Correct answers for vehicle registration and insurance exam 4

**1. B** (Comprehensive insurance)

**2. B** (Within 30 days)

**3. A** (To cover medical expenses for injuries sustained in a car accident)

**4. C** ($15,000)

**5. A** (Seek coverage from a different insurance company)

**6. A** (Annually)

**7. A** (To protect against damage to your vehicle from non-collision events)

**8. B** (Within 10 days)

**9. A** (Proof of insurance coverage)

**10. A** (Fines, suspension of driving privileges, and possible vehicle impoundment)

**11. A** (Within 10 days)

**12. A** (To protect you financially if you are involved in an accident with an uninsured driver)

**13. A** (Within 10 days)

**14. A** (To cover damage to your own vehicle caused by a collision with another vehicle or object)

**15. A** (Fines and possible suspension of driving privileges)

# Vehicle registration and insurance exam 5

**1. Which document must you present when registering a vehicle in Minnesota?**

A. ▢ Insurance card

B. ▢ Driver's license

C. ▢ Vehicle title

D. ▢ Vehicle inspection report

**2. What is the purpose of having liability insurance coverage?**

A. ▢ To protect your vehicle against theft or vandalism

B. ▢ To cover medical expenses for injuries sustained in a car accident

C. ▢ To provide coverage for rental vehicles

D. ▢ To protect you financially if you cause an accident and are at fault

**3. How often must you update your insurance information with the Minnesota Motor Vehicle Commission (MVC)?**

A. ▢ Annually

B. ▢ Every 2 years

C. ▢ Every 5 years

D. ▢ No need to update insurance information with the MVC

**4. What should you do if your insurance policy is canceled?**

A. ▢ Continue driving without insurance

B. ▢ Seek coverage from a different insurance company

C. ▢ Notify the MVC and surrender your driver's license

D. ▢ Ignore the cancellation and hope for the best

**5. When should you notify your insurance company about a change of vehicle ownership?**

A. ▢ Within 10 days

B. ▢ Within 30 days

C. ▢ Within 60 days

D. ▢ No need to notify the insurance company

**6. What is the minimum amount of liability insurance coverage required for bodily injury per person in Minnesota?**

A. ▢ $10,000

B. ▢ $15,000

C. ▢ $25,000

D. ▢ $50,000

**7. What is the purpose of having underinsured motorist coverage on your insurance policy?**

A. ▢ To protect you financially if you are involved in an accident with an underinsured driver

B. ▢ To cover medical expenses for injuries sustained in a car accident

C. ▢ To provide coverage for rental vehicles

D. ▢ Underinsured motorist coverage is not required in Minnesota

**8. How long do you have to renew your vehicle registration in Minnesota after it expires?**

A. ▢ 10 days

B. ▢ 30 days

C. ▢ 60 days

D. ▢ 90 days

**9. What is the purpose of having rental reimbursement coverage on your insurance policy?**

A. ▢ To cover the cost of rental vehicles while your vehicle is being repaired

B. ▢ To provide coverage for medical expenses in case of an accident

C. ▢ To protect against damage to your vehicle from non-collision events

D. ▢ Rental reimbursement coverage is not available in Minnesota

**10. What is the penalty for driving without valid insurance in Minnesota?**

A. ▢ Fines, suspension of driving privileges, and possible vehicle impoundment

B. ▢ Verbal warning from law enforcement

C. ▢ Reduction in vehicle registration fees

D. ▢ No penalty, as insurance coverage is not required in Minnesota

**11. When should you notify your insurance company about a change of address?**

A. ▢ Within 10 days

B. ▢ Within 30 days

C. ▢ Within 60 days

D. ▢ No need to notify the insurance company

**12. What is the purpose of having collision coverage on your insurance policy?**

A. ▢ To cover damage to your own vehicle caused by a collision with another vehicle or object

B. ▢ To protect against damage to your vehicle from non-collision events

C. ▢ To provide coverage for rental vehicles

D. ▢ Collision coverage is not required in Minnesota

**13. How long do you have to report a change of insurance provider to the Minnesota MVC?**

A. ▢ Within 10 days

B. ▢ Within 30 days

C. ▢ Within 60 days

D. ▢ No need to report a change of insurance provider to the MVC

**14. What is the purpose of having comprehensive insurance coverage?**

A. ▢ To protect your vehicle against damage from non-collision events, such as theft or vandalism

B. ▢ To cover medical expenses for injuries sustained in a car accident

C. ▢ To provide coverage for rental vehicles

D. ▢ Comprehensive insurance coverage is not required in Minnesota

**15. What is the penalty for driving with an expired vehicle registration in Minnesota?**

A. ▢ Fines and possible suspension of driving privileges

B. ▢ Verbal warning from law enforcement

C. ▢ Reduction in vehicle insurance premiums

D. ▢ No penalty, as vehicle registration is not required in Minnesota

# Correct answers for vehicle registration and insurance exam 5

**1. C** (Vehicle title)

**2. D** (To protect you financially if you cause an accident and are at fault)

**3. A** (Annually)

**4. B** (Seek coverage from a different insurance company)

**5. A** (Within 10 days)

**6. C** ($25,000)

**7. A** (To protect you financially if you are involved in an accident with an underinsured driver)

**8. B** (30 days)

**9. A** (To cover the cost of rental vehicles while your vehicle is being repaired)

**10. A** (Fines, suspension of driving privileges, and possible vehicle impoundment)

**11. B** (Within 30 days)

**12. A** (To cover damage to your own vehicle caused by a collision with another vehicle or object)

**13. A** (Within 10 days)

**14. A** (To protect your vehicle against damage from non-collision events, such as theft or vandalism)

**15. A** (Fines and possible suspension of driving privileges)

# Emergencies

Welcome to Chapter 8 of the Minnesota DMV Exam Workbook, where we explore the critical topic of emergencies. In this chapter, we will delve into the importance of preparedness and safe response in various emergency situations that can occur on the road. Understanding how to handle emergencies effectively is not only essential for passing your DMV exam but also for ensuring your safety, the safety of others, and minimizing the impact of unforeseen events on the road.

Emergencies can happen at any time while driving, and being prepared can make a significant difference in how effectively they are managed. This section will emphasize the importance of emergency preparedness and highlight the benefits of being proactive in anticipating and planning for potential emergencies. By understanding the significance of preparedness, you can act swiftly and confidently when faced with unexpected situations on the road.

## Common Roadside Emergencies

This section will explore some of the common roadside emergencies that drivers may encounter. From vehicle breakdowns and tire blowouts to engine overheating and fuel-related issues, understanding the causes, warning signs, and appropriate responses to these emergencies is vital. We will provide practical tips for minimizing risks, summoning assistance, and taking necessary precautions to ensure your safety and the safety of others.

## Accident Response and Safety Procedures

Being involved in a traffic accident is a stressful and potentially dangerous situation. This section will guide you through the necessary steps to follow in the event of an accident. We will discuss the importance of prioritizing safety, assessing injuries, contacting emergency services, documenting the incident, and exchanging information with other parties involved.

Understanding the appropriate accident response procedures will help mitigate further risks and ensure a smoother resolution.

## Medical Emergencies and First Aid

Encountering a medical emergency while on the road requires immediate action and potentially life-saving interventions. This section will cover the basics of first aid and provide an overview of common medical emergencies, such as heart attacks, seizures, and choking incidents. We will discuss the importance of recognizing the signs of distress, contacting emergency services, and providing appropriate assistance until professional help arrives.

## Hazardous Material Spills and Evacuation

Spills involving hazardous materials pose significant risks to drivers, passengers, and the environment. This section will outline the appropriate response procedures in the event of a hazardous material spill or leak. We will discuss the importance of notifying authorities, evacuating the area if necessary, and following safety protocols to minimize exposure and prevent further harm. Understanding the dangers associated with hazardous materials and knowing how to respond appropriately can save lives and protect the environment.

## Severe Weather and Natural Disasters

Driving in severe weather conditions or encountering natural disasters presents unique challenges and risks. This section will provide guidance on how to navigate these situations safely. We will discuss strategies for driving in adverse weather, such as heavy rain, snowstorms, or fog. Additionally, we will explore the necessary precautions to take when encountering natural disasters like hurricanes, tornadoes, or wildfires. By understanding the risks and taking appropriate actions, you can protect yourself and others from harm during severe weather events.

**Study Strategies for Emergency Preparedness**

To effectively prepare for the Minnesota DMV exam, it is important to implement study strategies specific to emergency preparedness. This section will provide you with practical tips for studying the material, such as reviewing emergency response procedures, familiarizing yourself with basic first aid techniques, and practicing decision-making skills in various emergency scenarios.

## Conclusion

As you progress on your journey toward becoming a licensed driver in Minnesota, remember that emergencies can happen when least expected. By prioritizing preparedness, equipping yourself with knowledge and skills, and remaining calm and focused, you can effectively respond to emergencies on the road. Your actions can make a significant difference in the outcome of these situations and contribute to the overall safety of yourself and others.

In the upcoming chapters, we will continue to explore crucial aspects of driving knowledge, including defensive driving techniques, road signs and signals, and hazard perception. Each chapter will build upon the foundation established in this introductory chapter, equipping you with the skills and knowledge needed to navigate Minnesota's roads responsibly and confidently.

Stay vigilant, prepared, and let's continue this journey toward becoming a skilled and responsible driver who can confidently handle emergencies on the road.

For training purposes, you can mark the ▫ symbol next to what you think is the correct answer: Once you have chosen the correct answer, use a pencil or pen to mark the ▫ symbol next to that answer.

So, let's get started!

# Emergencies exam

**1. In case of a vehicle fire, what should you NOT do?**

A. ▢ Pour water on the fire

B. ▢ Use a fire extinguisher, if available

C. ▢ Move away from the vehicle

D. ▢ Call emergency services


**2. What is the first thing you should do if you witness a collision?**

A. ▢ Provide first aid to the injured

B. ▢ Call emergency services

C. ▢ Move the vehicles out of the road

D. ▢ Take pictures of the accident scene


**3. When approaching a railroad crossing with flashing lights and gates down, what should you do?**

A. ▢ Stop at least 15 feet away from the crossing

B. ▢ Slow down and proceed with caution

C. ▢ Speed up to clear the tracks quickly

D. ▢ Change lanes and bypass the crossing


**4. How far should you stay behind an emergency vehicle with flashing lights and sirens?**

A. ▢ 50 feet

B. ▢ 100 feet

C. ▢ 200 feet

D. ▢ 500 feet

**5. What should you do if you encounter a downed power line?**

A. ▢ Drive over it if you can't find an alternate route

B. ▢ Drive around it without touching it

C. ▢ Stay inside the vehicle and call emergency services

D. ▢ Touch the power line to see if it's still live

**6. What should you do if your brakes fail while driving?**

A. ▢ Pump the brakes repeatedly

B. ▢ Shift into neutral and apply the parking brake

C. ▢ Turn off the engine and coast to a stop

D. ▢ Honk the horn to alert other drivers

**7. What should you do if you encounter a deer crossing the road?**

A. ▢ Swerve to avoid the deer

B. ▢ Brake firmly and stay in your lane

C. ▢ Speed up to scare the deer away

D. ▢ Ignore the deer and continue driving

**8. How should you respond if your vehicle begins to skid on a slippery road?**

A. ▢ Slam on the brakes

B. ▢ Steer in the opposite direction of the skid

C. ▢ Accelerate to regain control

D. ▢ Maintain a firm grip on the steering wheel and steer in the direction you want to go

**9. What is the recommended way to check for traffic when exiting a blind driveway?**

A. ▢ Rely on mirrors and backup cameras

B. ▢ Sound the horn to alert other drivers

C. ▢ Open the vehicle door and look for approaching vehicles

D. ▢ Slowly inch forward until you can see oncoming traffic

**10. What should you do if your vehicle's accelerator becomes stuck?**

A. ▢ Panic and quickly turn off the ignition

B. ▢ Firmly apply the brakes and shift into neutral

C. ▢ Pull the emergency brake and come to a complete stop

D. ▢ Shake the accelerator pedal vigorously to unstick it

**11. How should you position your hands on the steering wheel during an emergency maneuver?**

A. ▢ 9 and 3 o'clock

B. ▢ 10 and 2 o'clock

C. ▢ 8 and 4 o'clock

D. ▢ 12 o'clock

**12. What should you do if you witness a hit-and-run collision?**

A. ▢ Chase the fleeing vehicle to get its license plate number

B. ▢ Provide first aid to the injured before calling the police

C. ▢ Note the license plate number and vehicle description, and report it to the police

D. ▢ Ignore the collision and continue driving

**13. What is the first step in providing first aid to a bleeding person?**

A. ▢ Apply direct pressure to the wound with a clean cloth

B. ▢ Elevate the injured body part

C. ▢ Administer CPR

D. ▢ Call emergency services

**14. What should you do if you encounter a large animal on the roadway?**

A. ▢ Swerve to avoid the animal

B. ▢ Brake firmly and stay in your lane

C. ▢ Flash your headlights to scare the animal away

D. ▢ Slow down and be prepared to stop if necessary

**15. What is the correct procedure to follow if your vehicle becomes submerged in water?**

A. ▢ Stay inside the vehicle and wait for rescue

B. ▢ Open the windows and swim to the surface

C. ▢ Break the windshield and escape through it

D. ▢ Unbuckle your seatbelt and exit through a window

# Correct answers for emergencies exam

**1. A** (Pour water on the fire)

**2. B** (Call emergency services)

**3. A** (Stop at least 15 feet away from the crossing)

**4. C** (200 feet)

**5. C** (Stay inside the vehicle and call emergency services)

**6. B** (Shift into neutral and apply the parking brake)

**7. B** (Brake firmly and stay in your lane)

**8. D** (Maintain a firm grip on the steering wheel and steer in the direction you want to go)

**9. C** (Open the vehicle door and look for approaching vehicles)

**10. B** (Firmly apply the brakes and shift into neutral)

**11. A** (9 and 3 o'clock)

**12. C** (Note the license plate number and vehicle description, and report it to the police)

**13. A** (Apply direct pressure to the wound with a clean cloth)

**14. B** (Brake firmly and stay in your lane)

**15. A** (Stay inside the vehicle and wait for rescue)

# Emergencies exam 2

**1. When approaching an intersection where the traffic lights are not functioning, what should you do?**

A. ▢ Treat it as a four-way stop sign intersection

B. ▢ Yield the right-of-way to vehicles on your right

C. ▢ Proceed through the intersection without stopping

D. ▢ Speed up to clear the intersection quickly

**2. What should you do if you witness a vehicle leaking a hazardous material?**

A. ▢ Call emergency services and report the situation

B. ▢ Stop your vehicle and approach the leaking vehicle

C. ▢ Drive closely behind the leaking vehicle to monitor it

D. ▢ Ignore the situation unless it poses an immediate danger

**3. If your vehicle becomes submerged in water, what should you do?**

A. ▢ Open the windows and swim to the surface

B. ▢ Stay inside the vehicle and wait for rescue

C. ▢ Attempt to break the windows and escape

D. ▢ Remove your seatbelt and swim to safety

**4. What should you do if you come across a traffic signal that is stuck on red?**

A. ▢ Treat it as a stop sign and proceed when safe

B. ▢ Slow down and proceed with caution

C. ▢ Change lanes to avoid the intersection

D. ▢ Ignore the signal and continue driving

**5. When passing a stopped emergency vehicle with its lights flashing, what should you do?**

A. ▢ Increase your speed to pass quickly

B. ▢ Move to the lane farthest away from the emergency vehicle

C. ▢ Maintain your speed and stay in your lane

D. ▢ Honk your horn to alert the emergency vehicle

**6. What should you do if you encounter a large animal crossing the road?**

A. ▢ Swerve to avoid the animal

B. ▢ Brake firmly and stay in your lane

C. ▢ Speed up to scare the animal away

D. ▢ Use your high beams to blind the animal

**7. What should you do if your vehicle breaks down on the highway?**

A. ▢ Park on the shoulder and turn on your hazard lights

B. ▢ Attempt to fix the issue yourself

C. ▢ Exit your vehicle and walk to the nearest exit

D. ▢ Call a tow truck and leave your vehicle unattended

**8. How should you respond if you encounter a vehicle traveling the wrong way on a one-way street?**

A. ▢ Flash your headlights to warn the driver

B. ▢ Change lanes and pass the vehicle quickly

C. ▢ Slow down and move to the right side of the road

D. ▢ Call emergency services and report the situation

**9. What should you do if you notice smoke coming from under the hood of your vehicle?**

A. ▢ Pour water on the engine to cool it down

B. ▢ Open the hood and attempt to fix the issue

C. ▢ Turn off the engine and evacuate the vehicle

D. ▢ Drive to the nearest service station for assistance

**10. How should you respond if your vehicle's tire blows out while driving?**

A. ▢ Slam on the brakes and come to a stop

B. ▢ Grip the steering wheel firmly and steer straight

C. ▢ Accelerate to maintain control of the vehicle

D. ▢ Swerve to the side of the road immediately

**11. What should you do if your vehicle's headlights suddenly stop working at night?**

A. ▢ Continue driving with caution

B. ▢ Turn on the high beams instead

C. ▢ Pull over to a safe location and get assistance

D. ▢ Use the emergency hazard lights instead

**12. How should you respond if you witness a vehicle rollover accident?**

A. ▢ Park your vehicle and approach the accident scene

B. ▢ Call emergency services and provide details of the accident

C. ▢ Honk your horn to alert other drivers of the accident

D. ▢ Drive around the accident and continue on your way

**13. What should you do if you are caught in a severe thunderstorm while driving?**

A. ▢ Pull over to the side of the road and wait it out

B. ▢ Turn on your hazard lights and continue driving

C. ▢ Speed up to reach your destination quickly

D. ▢ Find shelter and park your vehicle until the storm passes

**14. What should you do if you encounter a pedestrian who is visually impaired?**

A. ▢ Sound your horn to alert them of your presence

B. ▢ Yield the right-of-way and allow them to cross safely

C. ▢ Drive closely behind them to guide them across the road

D. ▢ Speed up and pass them quickly

**15. How should you respond if your vehicle's gas pedal becomes stuck?**

A. ▢ Apply the brakes firmly and shift into neutral

B. ▢ Turn off the ignition and coast to a stop

C. ▢ Pump the gas pedal to unstick it

D. ▢ Use your hand to push the gas pedal back up

# Correct answers for emergencies exam 2

**1. A.** Treat it as a four-way stop sign intersection

**2. A.** Call emergency services and report the situation

**3. B**. Stay inside the vehicle and wait for rescue

**4. A.** Treat it as a stop sign and proceed when safe

**5. B.** Move to the lane farthest away from the emergency vehicle

**6. B**. Brake firmly and stay in your lane

**7. A.** Park on the shoulder and turn on your hazard lights

**8. C**. Slow down and move to the right side of the road

**9. C.** Turn off the engine and evacuate the vehicle

**10. B.** Grip the steering wheel firmly and steer straight

**11. C.** Pull over to a safe location and get assistance

**12. B.** Call emergency services and provide details of the accident

**13. A**. Pull over to the side of the road and wait it out

**14. B.** Yield the right-of-way and allow them to cross safely

**15. A.** Apply the brakes firmly and shift into neutral

# Emergencies exam 3

**1. What is the first thing you should do when you witness a car accident?**

A. ▢ Stop your vehicle and offer assistance

B. ▢ Call emergency services to report the accident

C. ▢ Honk your horn to alert other drivers

D. ▢ Drive away and continue on your route

**2. When should you activate your vehicle's hazard lights in an emergency situation?**

A. ▢ When you need to stop on the shoulder of the road

B. ▢ When you want to warn other drivers of a potential hazard

C. ▢ When you are driving in heavy rain or fog

D. ▢ When you want to communicate with nearby pedestrians

**3. What should you do if you encounter a downed power line on the road?**

A. ▢ Drive over the power line and continue on your way

B. ▢ Attempt to move the power line out of the road

C. ▢ Stay in your vehicle and call emergency services

D. ▢ Ignore the power line and proceed with caution

**4. How should you approach a scene where emergency personnel are assisting injured individuals?**

A. ▢ Slow down and proceed with caution

B. ▢ Speed up to quickly pass the scene

C. ▢ Stop your vehicle and offer assistance

D. ▢ Change lanes to avoid the scene altogether

**5. What should you do if your vehicle's engine catches fire while driving?**

A. ▢ Immediately stop the vehicle and evacuate

B. ▢ Open the hood and pour water on the engine

C. ▢ Call a tow truck to remove the vehicle from the road

D. ▢ Drive to the nearest gas station for assistance

**6. What should you do if you encounter a road flooded with water?**

A. ▢ Drive through the flooded area at a high speed

B. ▢ Stop your vehicle and turn around if possible

C. ▢ Shift into a lower gear and continue driving

D. ▢ Speed up to quickly pass through the water

**7. What should you do if you witness a hit-and-run accident?**

A. ▢ Follow the fleeing vehicle to obtain its license plate number

B. ▢ Take photos or videos of the accident scene and vehicles involved

C. ▢ Stop your vehicle and offer assistance to the victim

D. ▢ Drive away and ignore the incident

**8. What is the correct way to respond to a tire blowout while driving?**

A. ▢ Grip the steering wheel firmly and steer in the opposite direction of the blowout

B. ▢ Slam on the brakes to bring the vehicle to an immediate stop

C. ▢ Accelerate to maintain control of the vehicle

D. ▢ Gradually release the accelerator and steer straight

**9. What should you do if your vehicle becomes submerged in water?**

A. ▢ Open the windows and swim out of the vehicle

B. ▢ Stay inside the vehicle until help arrives

C. ▢ Use a sharp object to break the windows and escape

D. ▢ Attempt to start the vehicle and drive out of the water

**10. When should you use the three-point turn maneuver?**

A. ▢ When you need to turn around on a narrow street

B. ▢ When you want to merge onto a busy highway

C. ▢ When you need to pass a slow-moving vehicle

D. ▢ When you approach a pedestrian crossing

**11. What should you do if your vehicle's brakes fail?**

A. ▢ Pump the brake pedal rapidly to build up pressure

B. ▢ Shift into a lower gear to slow down the vehicle

C. ▢ Apply the parking brake gradually to stop the vehicle

D. ▢ Steer into a safe area and apply the emergency brake

**12. What should you do if your vehicle starts to skid on a slippery road?**

A. ▢ Brake firmly and steer in the opposite direction of the skid

B. ▢ Turn the steering wheel in the direction of the skid

C. ▢ Slam on the brakes to come to a quick stop

D. ▢ Release the accelerator and steer in the direction you want to go

**13. How should you respond if you encounter an aggressive driver on the road?**

A. ○ Slow down and let the aggressive driver pass

B. ○ Tailgate the aggressive driver to show dominance

C. ○ Use hand gestures and honk to express frustration

D. ○ Ignore the aggressive driver and continue driving

**14. What should you do if you approach a railroad crossing with flashing lights and gates?**

A. ○ Proceed with caution and be prepared to stop

B. ○ Speed up to quickly cross the tracks before the train arrives

C. ○ Drive around the gates if there are no approaching trains

D. ○ Stop and wait until the lights stop flashing and the gates lift

**15. What should you do if you encounter a vehicle traveling the wrong way on a one-way street?**

A. ○ Honk your horn to alert the driver of their mistake

B. ○ Slow down and move to the right to avoid the vehicle

C. ○ Continue driving and let other drivers handle the situation

D. ○ Pull over to the side of the road and call the police

# Correct answers for emergencies exam 3

**1. B** - Call emergency services to report the accident

**2. B** - When you want to warn other drivers of a potential hazard

**3. C** - Stay in your vehicle and call emergency services

**4. A** - Slow down and proceed with caution

**5. A** - Immediately stop the vehicle and evacuate

**6. B** - Stop your vehicle and turn around if possible

**7. A** - Follow the fleeing vehicle to obtain its license plate number

**8. D** - Gradually release the accelerator and steer straight

**9. B** - Stay inside the vehicle until help arrives

**10. A** - When you need to turn around on a narrow street

**11. D** - Steer into a safe area and apply the emergency brake

**12. D** - Release the accelerator and steer in the direction you want to go

**13. A** - Slow down and let the aggressive driver pass

**14. A** - Proceed with caution and be prepared to stop

**15. D** - Pull over to the side of the road and call the police

# Emergencies exam 4

**1. What should you do if you witness a vehicle rollover accident?**

A. ▢ Call emergency services and provide details about the accident

B. ▢ Drive around the accident scene to avoid traffic congestion

C. ▢ Stop your vehicle and approach the rollover vehicle to assist

D. ▢ Honk your horn to alert other drivers about the accident

**2. When approaching a traffic signal that is malfunctioning and displaying no lights, what should you do?**

A. ▢ Treat it as a four-way stop intersection and proceed with caution

B. ▢ Speed up and quickly pass through the intersection

C. ▢ Stop your vehicle and wait for the signal to resume normal operation

D. ▢ Ignore the malfunction and continue driving through the intersection

**3. What should you do if your vehicle's accelerator becomes stuck while driving?**

A. ▢ Shift into neutral and use the brakes to slow down and stop the vehicle

B. ▢ Turn off the engine and pull over to the side of the road

C. ▢ Pump the accelerator pedal rapidly to loosen it

D. ▢ Steer into oncoming traffic to avoid a collision

**4. What should you do if you encounter a deer or large animal on the roadway?**

A. ▢ Swerve your vehicle to avoid hitting the animal

B. ▢ Slam on the brakes to come to a sudden stop

C. ▢ Maintain your lane and brake firmly to minimize impact

D. ▢ Honk your horn to scare the animal away

**5. When should you use your vehicle's headlights during the daytime?**

A. ▢ When driving in residential areas with heavy pedestrian traffic

B. ▢ When driving on rural roads with limited visibility

C. ▢ When driving on highways with heavy traffic congestion

D. ▢ When driving in clear weather conditions

**6. What should you do if your vehicle experiences a sudden tire blowout while driving?**

A. ▢ Maintain a firm grip on the steering wheel and keep the vehicle straight

B. ▢ Swerve to the side of the road to avoid other vehicles

C. ▢ Apply the brakes hard to quickly come to a stop

D. ▢ Pump the brakes rapidly to regain control of the vehicle

**7. When should you use your vehicle's horn while driving?**

A. ▢ To alert other drivers of your presence in a dangerous situation

B. ▢ To express frustration or annoyance at other drivers

C. ▢ To greet friends or acquaintances on the road

D. ▢ To encourage pedestrians to hurry across the road

**8. What should you do if you encounter a bicyclist on the road?**

A. ▢ Maintain a safe distance and pass the bicyclist when it is safe to do so

B. ▢ Honk your horn to warn the bicyclist of your presence

C. ▢ Speed up to pass the bicyclist quickly and avoid holding up traffic

D. ▢ Follow closely behind the bicyclist to provide protection

**9. What should you do if you experience a sudden medical emergency while driving?**

A. ▢ Pull over to the side of the road and seek immediate medical attention

B. ▢ Continue driving and try to reach your destination as quickly as possible

C. ▢ Take over-the-counter medication to alleviate symptoms while driving

D. ▢ Ignore the symptoms and continue driving cautiously

**10. How should you respond if your vehicle becomes partially submerged in water?**

A. ▢ Open the windows and exit the vehicle immediately

B. ▢ Wait for help to arrive while remaining inside the vehicle

C. ▢ Attempt to restart the vehicle and drive out of the water

D. ▢ Disconnect the battery to prevent electrical damage

**11. What should you do if you witness a vehicle fire on the road?**

A. ▢ Call emergency services and provide details about the location and situation

B. ▢ Drive around the fire to avoid the potential danger

C. ▢ Approach the vehicle with a fire extinguisher to put out the fire

D. ▢ Honk your horn to alert other drivers about the fire

**12. When should you activate your vehicle's hazard lights?**

A. ▢ When your vehicle is stopped or disabled on the roadway

B. ▢ When you want to signal a turn or lane change

C. ▢ When driving in adverse weather conditions

D. ▢ When your vehicle is parked legally on the side of the road

**13. What should you do if you witness a hit-and-run accident?**

A. ▢ Note down the license plate number and provide it to the authorities

B. ▢ Chase the fleeing vehicle to obtain more information

C. ▢ Ignore the situation and continue driving

D. ▢ Alert other drivers about the accident by flashing your headlights


**14. How should you respond if your vehicle's hood suddenly flies open while driving?**

A. ▢ Maintain a firm grip on the steering wheel and slowly come to a stop

B. ▢ Accelerate to create wind pressure and force the hood back down

C. ▢ Slam on the brakes to come to an immediate stop

D. ▢ Steer your vehicle towards the side of the road to avoid collisions


**15. What should you do if your vehicle's windshield suddenly cracks or shatters while driving?**

A. ▢ Slow down and cautiously maneuver to the side of the road

B. ▢ Ignore the situation and continue driving at the same speed

C. ▢ Open the windows to equalize the air pressure and prevent further damage

D. ▢ Activate your vehicle's hazard lights to warn other drivers

# Correct answers for emergencies exam 4

**1. A** - Call emergency services and provide details about the accident

**2. A** - Treat it as a four-way stop intersection and proceed with caution

**3. A** - Shift into neutral and use the brakes to slow down and stop the vehicle

**4. C** - Maintain your lane and brake firmly to minimize impact

**5. B** - When driving on rural roads with limited visibility

**6. A** - Maintain a firm grip on the steering wheel and keep the vehicle straight

**7. A** - To alert other drivers of your presence in a dangerous situation

**8. A** - Maintain a safe distance and pass the bicyclist when it is safe to do so

**9. A** - Pull over to the side of the road and seek immediate medical attention

**10. A** - Open the windows and exit the vehicle immediately

**11. A** - Call emergency services and provide details about the location and situation

**12. A** - When your vehicle is stopped or disabled on the roadway

**13. A** - Note down the license plate number and provide it to the authorities

**14. A** - Maintain a firm grip on the steering wheel and slowly come to a stop

**15. A** - Slow down and cautiously maneuver to the side of the road

# Emergencies exam 5

**1. What should you do if you encounter a downed power line on the roadway?**

A. ▢ Drive over the power line to avoid causing traffic congestion

B. ▢ Stay inside your vehicle and call emergency services

C. ▢ Exit your vehicle and move the power line out of the way

D. ▢ Honk your horn to alert others about the danger

**2. When should you use your hazard lights while driving in an emergency situation?**

A. ▢ When your vehicle is stopped on the shoulder of the road

B. ▢ When you want to signal a turn or lane change

C. ▢ When driving in heavy rain or fog

D. ▢ When you are running late for an appointment

**3. What should you do if you witness a severe car crash on the highway?**

A. ▢ Call emergency services and provide details about the crash

B. ▢ Continue driving to avoid getting involved

C. ▢ Record the scene on your phone for social media

D. ▢ Drive closer to get a better look at the crash

**4. How should you respond if your vehicle's brakes fail while driving?**

A. ▢ Downshift to a lower gear and use the emergency brake to slow down

B. ▢ Panic and swerve off the road to avoid a collision

C. ▢ Pump the brakes rapidly to regain pressure

D. ▢ Turn off the engine and call for a tow truck

**5. What should you do if you encounter a traffic signal that is completely blacked out?**

A. ○ Treat it as a four-way stop intersection and proceed with caution

B. ○ Ignore it and continue driving through the intersection

C. ○ Speed up to pass through the intersection quickly

D. ○ Flash your high beams to alert other drivers

**6. When should you activate your vehicle's emergency flashers?**

A. ○ When your vehicle is stopped on the roadway due to mechanical issues

B. ○ When you want to signal to other drivers that you are in a hurry

C. ○ When you are driving in a funeral procession

D. ○ When you want to indicate your vehicle's location to emergency responders

**7. What should you do if you witness a person experiencing a medical emergency on the sidewalk?**

A. ○ Call emergency services and provide details about the situation

B. ○ Honk your horn to alert others about the situation

C. ○ Drive around the person to continue on your way

D. ○ Offer the person a ride to the nearest hospital

**8. How should you respond if your vehicle's accelerator becomes stuck while driving?**

A. ○ Shift into neutral and use the brakes to slow down and stop the vehicle

B. ○ Turn off the engine and come to a stop on the side of the road

C. ○ Kick the accelerator pedal to loosen it

D. ○ Steer into oncoming traffic to avoid a collision

**9. What should you do if you witness a building on fire near the roadway?**

A. ▢ Call emergency services and provide details about the location and situation

B. ▢ Drive closer to get a better look at the fire

C. ▢ Ignore the situation and continue driving

D. ▢ Record a video and post it on social media

**10. How should you respond if you encounter a road covered in black ice?**

A. ▢ Slow down and drive with caution, avoiding sudden acceleration or braking

B. ▢ Speed up to get through the icy section quickly

C. ▢ Steer into the skid and accelerate to gain control

D. ▢ Turn off the engine and wait for help to arrive

**11. What should you do if you witness a person trapped inside a locked car on a hot day?**

A. ▢ Call emergency services and provide details about the situation

B. ▢ Break the car window to rescue the person immediately

C. ▢ Ignore the situation and continue on your way

D. ▢ Honk your horn to alert others about the situation

**12. When should you activate your vehicle's fog lights?**

A. ▢ When driving in thick fog that reduces visibility

B. ▢ When you want to create a cool lighting effect on your vehicle

C. ▢ When you are driving at night on a well-lit road

D. ▢ When you want to signal to other drivers that you are in a hurry

**13. What should you do if you witness a severe thunderstorm while driving?**

A. ▢ Pull over to a safe location and wait until the storm passes

B. ▢ Drive faster to outrun the storm

C. ▢ Roll down your windows to enjoy the cool breeze

D. ▢ Continue driving normally, ignoring the storm

**14. How should you respond if your vehicle's steering becomes unresponsive while driving?**

A. ▢ Maintain a firm grip on the steering wheel and steer in the intended direction

B. ▢ Panic and jump out of the moving vehicle

C. ▢ Turn off the engine and call for a tow truck

D. ▢ Text a friend for advice on what to do

**15. What should you do if you witness a large animal crossing the road ahead of you?**

A. ▢ Slow down and be prepared to stop, as more animals may be following

B. ▢ Speed up to scare the animal away from the road

C. ▢ Honk your horn repeatedly to scare the animal

D. ▢ Swerve into the opposite lane to avoid the animal

# Correct answers for emergencies exam 5

**1. B** - Stay inside your vehicle and call emergency services

**2. A** - When your vehicle is stopped on the shoulder of the road

**3. A** - Call emergency services and provide details about the crash

**4. A** - Downshift to a lower gear and use the emergency brake to slow down

**5. A** - Treat it as a four-way stop intersection and proceed with caution

**6. A** - When your vehicle is stopped on the roadway due to mechanical issues

**7. A** - Call emergency services and provide details about the situation

**8. A** - Shift into neutral and use the brakes to slow down and stop the vehicle

**9. A** - Call emergency services and provide details about the location and situation

**10. A** - Slow down and drive with caution, avoiding sudden acceleration or braking

**11. A** - Call emergency services and provide details about the situation

**12. A** - When driving in thick fog that reduces visibility

**13. A** - Pull over to a safe location and wait until the storm passes

**14. A** - Maintain a firm grip on the steering wheel and steer in the intended direction

**15. A** - Slow down and be prepared to stop, as more animals may be following

# Vehicle size and weight limits

Welcome to Chapter 7 of the Minnesota DMV Exam Workbook, where we explore the essential topics of vehicle registration and insurance. In this chapter, we will delve into the requirements, processes, and importance of vehicle registration and insurance in the state of Minnesota. Understanding the legal obligations and financial protections associated with vehicle ownership is crucial for responsible and compliant driving.

Vehicle registration is a legal requirement that ensures accountability, traceability, and the proper identification of vehicles on Minnesota's roads. This section will emphasize the significance of vehicle registration, highlighting the role it plays in maintaining accurate records, facilitating law enforcement, and protecting public safety. By registering your vehicle, you contribute to the overall integrity and efficiency of the state's transportation system.

## Vehicle Registration Process

This section will provide a comprehensive overview of the vehicle registration process in Minnesota. We will explore the necessary documentation, such as proof of ownership, title transfer, and vehicle identification number (VIN) verification. We will also discuss the fees associated with registration and the importance of renewing registration on time to avoid penalties.

## License Plates and Registration Stickers

License plates and registration stickers serve as visual identifiers for registered vehicles. This section will cover the design, placement, and requirements for license plates and registration stickers in Minnesota. We will discuss the significance of properly displaying these identifiers and the consequences of tampering or unauthorized use.

## Vehicle Insurance Requirements

Vehicle insurance is a crucial aspect of responsible vehicle ownership, providing financial protection in the event of accidents, damage, or injuries. This section will explore the insurance requirements for vehicle owners in Minnesota. We will discuss the types of coverage available, such as liability, comprehensive, and collision, and the minimum coverage limits mandated by law. Understanding insurance requirements helps ensure financial security and compliance with state regulations.

## Proof of Insurance

This section will outline the importance of carrying proof of insurance while operating a vehicle in Minnesota. We will explore the acceptable forms of proof, such as insurance cards, digital copies, or electronic verification. Additionally, we will discuss the consequences of failing to provide proof of insurance when requested by law enforcement or during vehicle registration.

## Insurance Claims and Reporting Accidents

In the unfortunate event of an accident, understanding the insurance claims process is crucial. This section will provide an overview of the steps to take when filing an insurance claim and reporting accidents to your insurance company. We will discuss the importance of timely reporting, gathering evidence, and cooperating with insurance adjusters to expedite the claims process.

## Uninsured and Underinsured Motorist Coverage

Uninsured and underinsured motorist coverage is an additional layer of protection for vehicle owners in Minnesota. This section will explain the importance of this coverage, especially in situations where the at-fault party lacks sufficient insurance coverage. We will explore the benefits of uninsured and underinsured motorist coverage and the options available to vehicle owners in Minnesota.

## Vehicle Registration and Insurance Renewal

Renewal of vehicle registration and insurance policies is essential for maintaining compliance and continuous coverage. This section will discuss the renewal processes for both vehicle registration and insurance in Minnesota. We will emphasize the importance of timely renewals to avoid penalties, gaps in coverage, and potential legal consequences.

## Vehicle Registration and Insurance Fraud

Vehicle registration and insurance fraud pose significant risks to individuals, the insurance industry, and society as a whole. This section will explore common types of fraud, such as providing false information, staged accidents, or insurance scams. We will highlight the consequences of engaging in fraudulent activities and the importance of reporting any suspicions or incidents of fraud.

## Conclusion

By understanding the requirements and processes associated with vehicle registration and insurance, you are taking proactive steps towards responsible vehicle ownership and compliance with Minnesota's laws. Throughout this chapter, we will delve deeper into the specific aspects of vehicle registration and insurance, providing you with the knowledge and resources necessary to navigate the registration process, select appropriate insurance coverage, and ensure financial protection. So, let's embark on this journey of legal compliance and financial security, fostering responsible vehicle ownership in the Land of 10,000 Lakes.

For training purposes, you can mark the ▢ symbol next to what you think is the correct answer: Once you have chosen the correct answer, use a pencil or pen to mark the ▢ symbol next to that answer.

So, let's get started!

# Vehicle size and weight limits exam

**1. What is the maximum width allowed for a passenger vehicle in Minnesota?**

A. ▢ 6 feet

B. ▢ 7 feet

C. ▢ 8 feet

D. ▢ 9 feet

**2. What is the maximum weight allowed for a single axle on a commercial vehicle without a special permit?**

A. ▢ 10,000 pounds

B. ▢ 12,000 pounds

C. ▢ 15,000 pounds

D. ▢ 18,000 pounds

**3. What is the maximum height allowed for a commercial vehicle without a special permit?**

A. ▢ 12 feet

B. ▢ 13 feet

C. ▢ 14 feet

D. ▢ 15 feet

**4. What is the maximum weight allowed for a commercial vehicle without an overweight permit?**

A. ▢ 40,000 pounds

B. ▢ 50,000 pounds

C. ▢ 60,000 pounds

D. ▢ 70,000 pounds

**5. What is the maximum length allowed for a single vehicle in Minnesota?**

A. ▢ 30 feet

B. ▢ 35 feet

C. ▢ 40 feet

D. ▢ 45 feet

**6. What is the maximum weight allowed for a commercial vehicle on a Minnesota interstate highway without a special permit?**

A. ▢ 70,000 pounds

B. ▢ 80,000 pounds

C. ▢ 90,000 pounds

D. ▢ 100,000 pounds

**7. Which of the following vehicles may be subject to special permits for oversized loads?**

A. ▢ Passenger vehicles

B. ▢ Commercial trucks

C. ▢ Motorcycles

D. ▢ Bicycles

**8. What is the maximum weight allowed for a commercial vehicle on a Minnesota state highway without a special permit?**

A. ▢ 70,000 pounds

B. ▢ 80,000 pounds

C. ▢ 90,000 pounds

D. ▢ 100,000 pounds

**9. What is the maximum length allowed for a combination of vehicles (e.g., truck and trailer) in Minnesota?**

A. ▢ 50 feet

B. ▢ 60 feet

C. ▢ 70 feet

D. ▢ 80 feet

**10. Which of the following factors can affect the weight limit of a bridge or overpass?**

A. ▢ Weather conditions

B. ▢ Time of day

C. ▢ Age of the vehicle

D. ▢ Height of the vehicle

**11. What is the maximum weight allowed for a commercial vehicle on a Minnesota county road without a special permit?**

A. ▢ 40,000 pounds

B. ▢ 50,000 pounds

C. ▢ 60,000 pounds

D. ▢ 70,000 pounds

**12. What is the maximum width allowed for a commercial vehicle without a special permit?**

A. ▢ 8 feet

B. ▢ 9 feet

C. ▢ 10 feet

D. ▢ 11 feet

**13. What is the maximum length allowed for a commercial vehicle without a special permit?**

A. ▫ 40 feet

B. ▫ 45 feet

C. ▫ 50 feet

D. ▫ 55 feet

**14. Which of the following vehicles are generally exempt from size and weight restrictions?**

A. ▫ Emergency vehicles

B. ▫ School buses

C. ▫ Commercial delivery trucks

D. ▫ Personal passenger vehicles

**15. What is the maximum weight allowed for a combination of vehicles (e.g., truck and trailer) without an overweight permit?**

A. ▫ 80,000 pounds

B. ▫ 90,000 pounds

C. ▫ 100,000 pounds

D. ▫ 110,000 pounds

# Correct answers for vehicle size and weight limits exam

**1. B** - 7 feet

**2. C** - 15,000 pounds

**3. B** - 13 feet

**4. B** - 50,000 pounds

**5. D** - 45 feet

**6. B** - 80,000 pounds

**7. B** - Commercial trucks

**8. A** - 70,000 pounds

**9. C** - 70 feet

**10. D** - Height of the vehicle

**11. C** - 60,000 pounds

**12. A** - 8 feet

**13. C** - 50 feet

**14. A** - Emergency vehicles

**15. A** - 80,000 pounds

# Vehicle size and weight limits exam 2

**1. What is the maximum weight allowed for a single axle on a passenger vehicle in Minnesota?**

A. ▢ 4,000 pounds

B. ▢ 5,000 pounds

C. ▢ 6,000 pounds

D. ▢ 7,000 pounds

**2. What is the maximum weight allowed for a commercial truck with three axles without a special permit?**

A. ▢ 48,000 pounds

B. ▢ 54,000 pounds

C. ▢ 60,000 pounds

D. ▢ 66,000 pounds

**3. What is the maximum width allowed for a combination of vehicles (e.g., truck and trailer) in New  Jersey?**

A. ▢ 8 feet

B. ▢ 8.5 feet

C. ▢ 9 feet

D. ▢ 9.5 feet

**4. What is the maximum weight allowed for a commercial truck with six or more axles without a special permit?**

A. ▢ 78,000 pounds

B. ▢ 80,000 pounds

C. ▢ 82,000 pounds

D. ▢ 84,000 pounds

**5. What is the maximum length allowed for a single trailer in a combination of vehicles without a special permit?**

A. ▢ 40 feet

B. ▢ 45 feet

C. ▢ 48 feet

D. ▢ 53 feet

**6. What is the maximum weight allowed for a recreational vehicle (RV) without a special permit?**

A. ▢ 10,000 pounds

B. ▢ 15,000 pounds

C. ▢ 20,000 pounds

D. ▢ 25,000 pounds

**7. Which of the following vehicles are required to have an overweight permit for operating on New Jersey roadways?**

A. ▢ Motorcycles

B. ▢ Personal passenger vehicles

C. ▢ Commercial trucks

D. ▢ Bicycles

**8. What is the maximum height allowed for a combination of vehicles (e.g., truck and trailer) without a special permit?**

A. ▢ 12 feet

B. ▢ 13 feet

C. ▢ 14 feet

D. ▢ 15 feet

**9. What is the maximum weight allowed for a single axle on a recreational vehicle (RV) without a special permit?**

A. ▢ 6,000 pounds

B. ▢ 7,000 pounds

C. ▢ 8,000 pounds

D. ▢ 9,000 pounds

**10. What is the maximum weight allowed for a combination of vehicles (e.g., truck and trailer) without an overweight permit?**

A. ▢ 60,000 pounds

B. ▢ 65,000 pounds

C. ▢ 70,000 pounds

D. ▢ 75,000 pounds

**11. What is the maximum length allowed for a commercial truck without a special permit?**

A. ▢ 50 feet

B. ▢ 55 feet

C. ▢ 60 feet

D. ▢ 65 feet

**12. Which of the following factors can affect the weight limit of a bridge or overpass?**

A. ▢ Vehicle speed

B. ▢ Road conditions

C. ▢ Time of day

D. ▢ Bridge structure and design

**13. What is the maximum weight allowed for a single axle on a commercial truck without a special permit?**

A. ▢ 12,000 pounds

B. ▢ 13,000 pounds

C. ▢ 14,000 pounds

D. ▢ 15,000 pounds

**14. Which of the following vehicles are generally exempt from size and weight restrictions?**

A. ▢ Emergency vehicles

B. ▢ School buses

C. ▢ Commercial delivery trucks

D. ▢ Personal passenger vehicles

**15. What is the maximum weight allowed for a combination of vehicles (e.g., truck and trailer) without an overweight permit?**

A. ▢ 80,000 pounds

B. ▢ 90,000 pounds

C. ▢ 100,000 pounds

D. ▢ 110,000 pounds

# Correct answers for vehicle size and weight limits exam 2

1. **B** - 5,000 pounds

2. **C** - 60,000 pounds

3. **B** - 8.5 feet

4. **B** - 80,000 pounds

5. **D** - 53 feet

6. **B** - 15,000 pounds

7. **C** - Commercial trucks

8. **B** - 13 feet

9. **A** - 6,000 pounds

10. **C** - 70,000 pounds

11. **B** - 55 feet

12. **D** - Bridge structure and design

13. **B** - 13,000 pounds

14. **A** - Emergency vehicles

15. **A** - 80,000 pounds

# Vehicle size and weight limits exam 3

**1. What is the maximum weight allowed for a single axle on a passenger vehicle in Minnesota?**

A. ▢ 4,500 pounds

B. ▢ 5,500 pounds

C. ▢ 6,500 pounds

D. ▢ 7,500 pounds

**2. What is the maximum weight allowed for a commercial truck with three axles without a special permit?**

A. ▢ 46,000 pounds

B. ▢ 52,000 pounds

C. ▢ 58,000 pounds

D. ▢ 64,000 pounds

**3. What is the maximum width allowed for a combination of vehicles (e.g., truck and trailer) in Minnesota?**

A. ▢ 8.2 feet

B. ▢ 8.8 feet

C. ▢ 9.4 feet

D. ▢ 10 feet

**4. What is the maximum weight allowed for a commercial truck with six or more axles without a special permit?**

A. ▫ 76,000 pounds

B. ▫ 78,000 pounds

C. ▫ 80,000 pounds

D. ▫ 82,000 pounds

**5. What is the maximum length allowed for a single trailer in a combination of vehicles without a special permit?**

A. ▫ 42 feet

B. ▫ 46 feet

C. ▫ 50 feet

D. ▫ 54 feet

**6. What is the maximum weight allowed for a recreational vehicle (RV) without a special permit?**

A. ▫ 12,000 pounds

B. ▫ 14,000 pounds

C. ▫ 16,000 pounds

D. ▫ 18,000 pounds

**7. Which of the following vehicles are required to have an overweight permit for operating on Minnesota roadways?**

A. ▫ Motorcycles

B. ▫ Personal passenger vehicles

C. ▫ Commercial trucks

D. ▫ Bicycles

**8. What is the maximum height allowed for a combination of vehicles (e.g., truck and trailer) without a special permit?**

A. ▢ 12.5 feet

B. ▢ 13.5 feet

C. ▢ 14.5 feet

D. ▢ 15.5 feet

**9. What is the maximum weight allowed for a single axle on a recreational vehicle (RV) without a special permit?**

A. ▢ 7,500 pounds

B. ▢ 8,500 pounds

C. ▢ 9,500 pounds

D. ▢ 10,500 pounds

**10. What is the maximum weight allowed for a combination of vehicles (e.g., truck and trailer) without an overweight permit?**

A. ▢ 62,000 pounds

B. ▢ 68,000 pounds

C. ▢ 74,000 pounds

D. ▢ 80,000 pounds

**11. What is the maximum length allowed for a commercial truck without a special permit?**

A. ▢ 56 feet

B. ▢ 60 feet

C. ▢ 64 feet

D. ▢ 68 feet

**12. Which of the following factors can affect the weight limit of a bridge or overpass?**

A. ▢ Vehicle speed

B. ▢ Road conditions

C. ▢ Weather conditions

D. ▢ Bridge structure and design

**13. What is the maximum weight allowed for a single axle on a commercial truck without a special permit?**

A. ▢ 12,000 pounds

B. ▢ 13,000 pounds

C. ▢ 14,000 pounds

D. ▢ 15,000 pounds

**14. Which of the following vehicles are generally exempt from size and weight restrictions?**

A. ▢ Emergency vehicles

B. ▢ School buses

C. ▢ Commercial delivery trucks

D. ▢ Personal passenger vehicles

**15. What is the maximum weight allowed for a combination of vehicles (e.g., truck and trailer) without an overweight permit?**

A. ▢ 80,000 pounds

B. ▢ 90,000 pounds

C. ▢ 100,000 pounds

D. ▢ 110,000 pounds

# Correct answers for vehicle size and weight limits exam 3

**1. A** - 4,500 pounds

**2. C** - 58,000 pounds

**3. D** - 10 feet

**4. C** - 80,000 pounds

**5. D** - 54 feet

**6. B** - 14,000 pounds

**7. C** - Commercial trucks

**8. B** - 13.5 feet

**9. A** - 7,500 pounds

**10. D** - 80,000 pounds

**11. B** - 60 feet

**12. D** - Bridge structure and design

**13. B** - 13,000 pounds

**14. A** - Emergency vehicles

**15. A** - 80,000 pounds

# Vehicle size and weight limits exam 4

1. What is the maximum width allowed for a vehicle operating without a special permit in Minnesota?

A. ▢ 7 feet

B. ▢ 8 feet

C. ▢ 9 feet

D. ▢ 10 feet

2. What is the maximum weight allowed for a commercial truck with four axles without a special permit?

A. ▢ 60,000 pounds

B. ▢ 64,000 pounds

C. ▢ 68,000 pounds

D. ▢ 72,000 pounds

3. What is the maximum length allowed for a combination of vehicles (e.g., truck and trailer) without an overweight permit?

A. ▢ 58 feet

B. ▢ 62 feet

C. ▢ 66 feet

D. ▢ 70 feet

**4. Which of the following vehicles are required to have a special permit for operating on Minnesota roadways?**

A. ▢ Motorcycles

B. ▢ Personal passenger vehicles

C. ▢ Oversized commercial trucks

D. ▢ Bicycles

**5. What is the maximum weight allowed for a recreational vehicle (RV) with two axles without a special permit?**

A. ▢ 18,000 pounds

B. ▢ 20,000 pounds

C. ▢ 22,000 pounds

D. ▢ 24,000 pounds

**6. What is the maximum height allowed for a combination of vehicles (e.g., truck and trailer) without an overweight permit?**

A. ▢ 14 feet

B. ▢ 14.5 feet

C. ▢ 15 feet

D. ▢ 15.5 feet

**7. Which of the following factors can affect the weight limit of a vehicle?**

A. ▢ Vehicle color

B. ▢ Vehicle model

C. ▢ Vehicle suspension

D. ▢ Vehicle speed

**8. What is the maximum weight allowed for a single axle on a commercial truck without a special permit?**

A. ▢ 16,000 pounds

B. ▢ 18,000 pounds

C. ▢ 20,000 pounds

D. ▢ 22,000 pounds

**9. What is the maximum weight allowed for a combination of vehicles (e.g., truck and trailer) without an overweight permit?**

A. ▢ 90,000 pounds

B. ▢ 95,000 pounds

C. ▢ 100,000 pounds

D. ▢ 105,000 pounds

**10. What is the maximum length allowed for a commercial truck with three axles without a special permit?**

A. ▢ 52 feet

B. ▢ 56 feet

C. ▢ 60 feet

D. ▢ 64 feet

**11. Which of the following vehicles are generally exempt from size and weight restrictions?**

A. ▢ Emergency vehicles

B. ▢ Taxis

C. ▢ Rental cars

D. ▢ Commercial delivery trucks

**12.** What is the maximum weight allowed for a single axle on a passenger vehicle without a special permit?

A. ▢ 5,000 pounds

B. ▢ 6,000 pounds

C. ▢ 7,000 pounds

D. ▢ 8,000 pounds

**13.** What is the maximum weight allowed for a recreational trailer without a special permit?

A. ▢ 10,000 pounds

B. ▢ 12,000 pounds

C. ▢ 14,000 pounds

D. ▢ 16,000 pounds

**14.** What is the maximum weight allowed for a combination of vehicles (e.g., truck and trailer) without an overweight permit?

A. ▢ 110,000 pounds

B. ▢ 115,000 pounds

C. ▢ 120,000 pounds

D. ▢ 125,000 pounds

**15.** What is the maximum length allowed for a passenger vehicle without a special permit?

A. ▢ 20 feet

B. ▢ 22 feet

C. ▢ 24 feet

D. ▢ 26 feet

# Correct answers for vehicle size and weight limits exam 4

**1. B** - 8 feet

**2. C** - 68,000 pounds

**3. A** - 58 feet

**4. C** - Oversized commercial trucks

**5. A** - 18,000 pounds

**6. B** - 14.5 feet

**7. C** - Vehicle suspension

**8. B** - 18,000 pounds

**9. A** - 90,000 pounds

**10. C** - 60 feet

**11. A** - Emergency vehicles

**12. A** - 5,000 pounds

**13. B** - 12,000 pounds

**14. C** - 120,000 pounds

**15. A** - 20 feet

# Vehicle size and weight limits exam 5

1. What is the maximum weight allowed for a commercial truck with five axles without a special permit?

A. ▢ 80,000 pounds

B. ▢ 84,000 pounds

C. ▢ 88,000 pounds

D. ▢ 92,000 pounds

2. What is the maximum width allowed for a recreational vehicle (RV) without a special permit?

A. ▢ 8 feet

B. ▢ 8.5 feet

C. ▢ 9 feet

D. ▢ 9.5 feet

3. Which of the following vehicles are required to display a "Wide Load" sign when operating on Minnesota roadways?

A. ▢ Motorcycles

B. ▢ Passenger cars

C. ▢ Oversized vehicles

D. ▢ Bicycles

**4. What is the maximum weight allowed for a single axle on a commercial truck with three axles without a special permit?**

A. ☐ 18,000 pounds

B. ☐ 20,000 pounds

C. ☐ 22,000 pounds

D. ☐ 24,000 pounds

**5. What is the maximum length allowed for a passenger vehicle with a trailer without a special permit?**

A. ☐ 40 feet

B. ☐ 42 feet

C. ☐ 44 feet

D. ☐ 46 feet

**6. What is the maximum weight allowed for a recreational trailer with two axles without a special permit?**

A. ☐ 14,000 pounds

B. ☐ 16,000 pounds

C. ☐ 18,000 pounds

D. ☐ 20,000 pounds

**7. What is the maximum height allowed for a commercial truck with two axles without a special permit?**

A. ☐ 13 feet

B. ☐ 13.5 feet

C. ☐ 14 feet

D. ▢ 14.5 feet

8. Which of the following vehicles are generally exempt from vehicle size and weight restrictions?

A. ▢ Public transit buses

B. ▢ Limousines

C. ▢ Commercial delivery vans

D. ▢ Rental cars

9. What is the maximum weight allowed for a single axle on a passenger vehicle with two axles without a special permit?

A. ▢ 3,000 pounds

B. ▢ 4,000 pounds

C. ▢ 5,000 pounds

D. ▢ 6,000 pounds

10. What is the maximum length allowed for a commercial truck with six axles without a special permit?

A. ▢ 68 feet

B. ▢ 70 feet

C. ▢ 72 feet

D. ▢ 74 feet

**11. What is the maximum weight allowed for a combination of vehicles (e.g., truck and trailer) without an overweight permit?**

A. ▢ 130,000 pounds

B. ▢ 135,000 pounds

C. ▢ 140,000 pounds

D. ▢ 145,000 pounds

**12. What is the maximum weight allowed for a single axle on a recreational vehicle (RV) without a special permit?**

A. ▢ 6,000 pounds

B. ▢ 7,000 pounds

C. ▢ 8,000 pounds

D. ▢ 9,000 pounds

**13. What is the maximum length allowed for a commercial truck with four axles without a special permit?**

A. ▢ 52 feet

B. ▢ 54 feet

C. ▢ 56 feet

D. ▢ 58 feet

**14. Which of the following vehicles are required to undergo weigh station inspections?**

A. ▢ School buses

B. ▢ Motorcycles

C. ▢ Electric vehicles

D. ▢ Private sedans

15. **What is the maximum weight allowed for a single axle on a recreational trailer without a special permit?**

A. ▢ 3,500 pounds

B. ▢ 4,500 pounds

C. ▢ 5,500 pounds

D. ▢ 6,500 pounds

# Correct answers for vehicle size and weight limits exam 5

1. **C** - 88,000 pounds

2. **A** - 8 feet

3. **C** - Oversized vehicles

4. **A** - 18,000 pounds

5. **C** - 44 feet

6. **C** - 18,000 pounds

7. **B** - 13.5 feet

8. **A -** Public transit buses

9. **B** - 4,000 pounds

10. **C** - 72 feet

11. **C** - 140,000 pounds

12. **A** - 6,000 pounds

13. **C** - 56 feet

14. **A** - School buses

15. **A** - 3,500 pounds

# Public transportation

Welcome to Chapter 10 of the Minnesota DMV Exam Workbook, where we delve into the dynamic world of public transportation. In this chapter, we explore the essential role of public transportation in enhancing mobility, reducing congestion, and promoting sustainable transportation options throughout the Land of 10,000 Lakes. Understanding the principles, benefits, and responsibilities associated with public transportation is vital for both drivers and passengers alike.

Public transportation plays a pivotal role in fostering a well-connected and sustainable transportation network. This section emphasizes the significance of public transportation in enhancing accessibility, reducing traffic congestion, mitigating environmental impacts, and promoting equitable transportation options. By embracing public transportation, individuals can contribute to creating a more efficient and sustainable transportation system in Minnesota.

## Public Transportation Modes and Services

This section provides an overview of various public transportation modes and services available in Minnesota. We will explore options such as buses, light rail, commuter trains, and paratransit services. Understanding the characteristics, benefits, and limitations of each mode will help individuals make informed choices when utilizing public transportation.

## Transit Planning and Infrastructure

Transit planning and infrastructure play a crucial role in developing a robust public transportation system. This section will discuss the principles and considerations involved in planning efficient transit routes, designing transit hubs, and providing necessary infrastructure, such as bus stops, train stations, and park-and-ride facilities. By investing in well-designed transit infrastructure, Minnesota aims to enhance accessibility and encourage greater public transportation usage.

## Public Transportation Safety and Security

Safety and security are paramount in public transportation systems. This section addresses the safety measures and protocols implemented to ensure passenger well-being, including surveillance systems, emergency response plans, and public awareness campaigns. We will also discuss passenger etiquette and the importance of being respectful and considerate of fellow passengers while using public transportation.

## Public Transportation Fare Systems and Payment Methods

Paying for public transportation services requires an understanding of fare systems and payment methods. This section will outline the different fare structures, such as flat fares and zone-based fares, as well as the available payment options, including cash, prepaid cards, and mobile applications. We will also highlight the importance of fare compliance and the consequences of fare evasion.

## Accessible and Inclusive Public Transportation

Public transportation should be accessible to all individuals, regardless of their physical abilities. This section will focus on the accessibility features and services provided by public transportation operators, such as wheelchair ramps, audio announcements, and priority seating. We will also discuss the responsibilities of both operators and passengers in ensuring an inclusive and accommodating environment.

## Public Transportation and the Environment

One of the significant advantages of public transportation is its positive impact on the environment. This section explores the environmental benefits of utilizing public transportation, including reduced greenhouse gas emissions, energy conservation, and improved air quality. We will highlight

Minnesota's commitment to sustainability and the role of public transportation in achieving environmental goals.

## Public Transportation Etiquette and Courtesy

Courtesy and respect are essential when using public transportation. This section will discuss proper etiquette, including queueing, giving up seats for those in need, and maintaining cleanliness. We will emphasize the importance of being mindful of fellow passengers and creating a positive and comfortable atmosphere for everyone.

## Public Transportation Challenges and Future Outlook

Despite its numerous benefits, public transportation also faces various challenges. This section will explore common challenges, such as funding limitations, infrastructure expansion, and ridership fluctuations. Additionally, we will discuss future advancements and initiatives aimed at improving public transportation systems in Minnesota, including the integration of technology, expansion of services, and fostering community engagement.

## Conclusion

By understanding the principles and benefits of public transportation, as well as the responsibilities of both passengers and operators, individuals can contribute to a sustainable and efficient transportation system in Minnesota. Throughout this chapter, we will delve into the intricacies of public transportation, empowering you with the knowledge to make informed choices and embrace the advantages of public transportation. So, let's embark on this journey of exploring public transportation and its transformative potential in the Land of 10,000 Lakes.

For training purposes, you can mark the ▢ symbol next to what you think is the correct answer: Once you have chosen the correct answer, use a pencil or pen to mark the ▢ symbol next to that answer.

# Public transportation exam

**1. Which of the following is considered a form of public transportation?**

A. ▢ Taxis

B. ▢ Personal cars

C. ▢ Rental bikes

D. ▢ Motorcycles

**2. What is the primary purpose of public transportation systems?**

A. ▢ Providing convenience for individual travelers

B. ▢ Promoting car ownership and usage

C. ▢ Reducing traffic congestion and pollution

D. ▢ Generating revenue for the government

**3. True or False: Public transportation vehicles are exempt from traffic laws and regulations.**

A. ▢ True

B. ▢ False

**4. Which of the following is an example of public transportation infrastructure?**

A. ▢ Sidewalks

B. ▢ Shopping malls

C. ▢ Airport terminals

D. ▢ Residential neighborhoods

**5. What is the purpose of designated bus lanes on roadways?**

A. ▢ Allowing buses to travel at higher speeds

B. ▢ Providing exclusive parking spaces for buses

C. ▢ Encouraging carpooling among commuters

D. ▢ Enabling faster delivery services

**6. Which agency is responsible for overseeing public transportation services in Minnesota?**

A. ▢ NJ Transit

B. ▢ Department of Motor Vehicles (DMV)

C. ▢ Federal Aviation Administration (FAA)

D. ▢ Environmental Protection Agency (EPA)

**7. True or False: Public transportation is only available in urban areas and not in rural areas.**

A. ▢ True

B. ▢ False

**8. What is the purpose of fare collection on public transportation systems?**

A. ▢ Funding maintenance and operations

B. ▢ Discouraging people from using public transportation

C. ▢ Generating profits for private companies

D. ▢ Increasing travel times for passengers

**9. Which of the following is an example of fixed-route public transportation?**

A. ▢ On-demand ride-sharing services

B. ▢ School buses

C. ▢ Intercity trains

D. ▢ Charter buses

**10. What is the primary mode of public transportation in Minnesota?**

A. ▢ Buses

B. ▢ Trains

C. ▢ Ferries

D. ▢ Light rail

**11. True or False: Public transportation systems are accessible to people with disabilities.**

A. ▢ True

B. ▢ False

**12. What is the purpose of park-and-ride facilities near public transportation stations?**

A. ▢ Providing additional parking spaces for commuters

B. ▢ Offering recreational activities for the public

C. ▢ Encouraging people to drive their own cars

D. ▢ Storing surplus public transportation vehicles

**13. Which of the following is a benefit of using public transportation?**

A. ○ Higher fuel costs

B. ○ Increased traffic congestion

C. ○ Lower greenhouse gas emissions

D. ○ Limited mobility options

**14. True or False: Public transportation is only available during specific hours of the day.**

A. ○ True

B. ○ False

**15. What is the purpose of transit-oriented development (TOD) projects?**

A. ○ Promoting private vehicle ownership

B. ○ Expanding road infrastructure

C. ○ Encouraging mixed-use development near transit stations

D. ○ Minimizing pedestrian and bicycle infrastructure

# Correct answers for public transportation exam

1. **A** - Taxis

2. **C** - Reducing traffic congestion and pollution

3. **B** - False

4. **C** - Airport terminals

5. **A** - Allowing buses to travel at higher speeds

6. **A** - NJ Transit

7. **B** - False

8. **A** - Funding maintenance and operations

9. **C** - Intercity trains

10. **A** - Buses

11. **A** - True

12. **A** - Providing additional parking spaces for commuters

13. **C** - Lower greenhouse gas emissions

14. **B** - False

15. **C** - Encouraging mixed-use development near transit stations

# Public transportation exam 2

1. Which of the following is a common feature of a well-designed public transportation system?

    A. ▢ Large parking lots for personal vehicles

    B. ▢ Accessible stations for people with disabilities

    C. ▢ Toll booths for collecting additional fees

    D. ▢ Limited service hours during weekdays

2. True or False: Public transportation systems help reduce traffic congestion and air pollution.

    A. ▢ True

    B. ▢ False

3. What is the purpose of a transfer ticket in public transportation?

    A. ▢ Granting priority seating to passengers

    B. ▢ Providing discounts for future trips

    C. ▢ Allowing passengers to switch between different routes

    D. ▢ Exempting passengers from fare collection

4. Which of the following is an example of a public transportation operator?

    A. ▢ City taxi service

    B. ▢ Rental car company

    C. ▢ Private limousine service

    D. ▢ Intercity bus company

**5. True or False: Public transportation is a cost-effective option for daily commuting.**

A. ▢ True

B. ▢ False

**6. What is the purpose of transit signal priority (TSP) for buses?**

A. ▢ Preventing buses from accessing bus stops

B. ▢ Enabling faster travel times for buses

C. ▢ Discouraging passengers from boarding buses

D. ▢ Increasing traffic congestion near bus routes

**7. Which of the following is a benefit of using public transportation for long-distance travel?**

A. ▢ Greater flexibility in travel schedules

B. ▢ Reduced travel time compared to driving

C. ▢ Lower fuel efficiency compared to personal vehicles

D. ▢ Higher overall travel costs

**8. True or False: Public transportation systems typically operate on fixed schedules.**

A. ▢ True

B. ▢ False

**9. What is the purpose of a dedicated bus lane on a roadway?**

A. ▢ Allowing private vehicles to use the lane

B. ▢ Providing exclusive parking spaces for buses

C. ▢ Facilitating faster and more reliable bus service

D. ▢ Encouraging pedestrians to use the lane

**10. Which government agency is responsible for regulating public transportation safety?**

A. ▢ Federal Transit Administration (FTA)

B. ▢ Department of Housing and Urban Development (HUD)

C. ▢ National Highway Traffic Safety Administration (NHTSA)

D. ▢ Environmental Protection Agency (EPA)

**11. True or False: Public transportation is primarily designed for short-distance trips within a city.**

A. ▢ True

B. ▢ False

**12. What is the purpose of a turnstile in a subway station?**

A. ▢ Collecting fares from passengers

B. ▢ Controlling pedestrian access to the station

C. ▢ Providing seating for waiting passengers

D. ▢ Displaying train schedules and information

**13. Which of the following is an example of a demand-responsive public transportation service?**

A. ▫ Commuter trains

B. ▫ Airport shuttles

C. ▫ Bike-sharing programs

D. ▫ Paratransit services for individuals with disabilities

**14. True or False: Public transportation systems are more energy-efficient compared to personal vehicles.**

A. ▫ True

B. ▫ False

**15. What is the purpose of a public transportation subsidy?**

A. ▫ Increasing fares for passengers

B. ▫ Discouraging people from using public transportation

C. ▫ Providing financial support to transit agencies

D. ▫ Expanding private transportation options

# Correct answers for public transportation exam 2

**1. B.** Accessible stations for people with disabilities

**2.** True

**3. C.** Transferring to another bus or train without an additional fee

**4. D.** All of the above

**5. A.** Park-and-ride lots

**6. B.** To provide information about the route and stops

**7. D.** All of the above

**8. A.** Lower cost compared to driving a private vehicle

**9. B.** Bus Rapid Transit (BRT)

**10. C.** Reducing traffic congestion and pollution

**11. D.** Provide transportation options for residents and visitors

**12. A.** True

**13. C.** Electric buses produce zero tailpipe emissions

**14. B.** Local transit agencies and departments of transportation

**15. C.** Providing financial support to transit agencies

# Public transportation exam 3

**1. What is the purpose of designated bus lanes on city streets?**

A. ▢ To provide additional parking spaces

B. ▢ To improve traffic flow for private vehicles

C. ▢ To ensure priority for buses and reduce travel time

D. ▢ To restrict public transportation access

**2. True or False: Public transportation systems are primarily designed for commuters and not suitable for other purposes.**

A. ▢ True

B. ▢ False

**3. What is a common benefit of using a smart card or electronic payment system for public transportation?**

A. ▢ Higher fare costs

B. ▢ Limited access to certain routes

C. ▢ Slower boarding process

D. ▢ Convenient and faster fare payment

**4. Which of the following is a form of public transportation?**

A. ▢ Taxi

B. ▢ Car rental service

C. ▢ Personal bicycle

D. ▢ Bus

**5. What does the term "fare evasion" refer to in the context of public transportation?**

A. ▢ Paying the correct fare amount

B. ▢ Using public transportation during peak hours

C. ▢ Boarding a bus from the front entrance

D. ▢ Avoiding paying the required fare

**6. How do designated bus stops contribute to efficient public transportation?**

A. ▢ They provide additional space for private vehicles

B. ▢ They encourage pedestrian traffic congestion

C. ▢ They help ensure orderly boarding and alighting of passengers

D. ▢ They are used exclusively for tourist buses

**7. Which of the following is a characteristic of a high-occupancy vehicle (HOV) lane?**

A. ▢ It is reserved for commercial vehicles only

B. ▢ It allows motorcycles to travel at higher speeds

C. ▢ It requires vehicles to have a minimum number of occupants

D. ▢ It is open only during non-peak hours

**8. True or False: Using public transportation can help reduce traffic congestion and air pollution.**

A. ▢ True

B. ▢ False

**9. What is the purpose of a transit signal priority system?**

A. ▢ To extend green signal time for private vehicles

B. ▢ To prioritize the movement of bicycles at intersections

C. ▢ To provide faster response times for emergency vehicles

D. ▢ To give buses priority at traffic signals for smoother flow

**10. When riding a bus, where should you wait to be picked up?**

A. ▢ In the middle of the road

B. ▢ On the sidewalk or designated bus stop

C. ▢ In a parking lot or private driveway

D. ▢ In front of a fire hydrant or crosswalk

**11. True or False: Public transportation is an affordable option for many individuals and can help save money on fuel and parking costs.**

A. ▢ True

B. ▢ False

**12. What should you do when boarding a crowded bus?**

A. ▢ Force your way through to find a seat

B. ▢ Wait for the next bus to arrive

C. ▢ Stand near the driver's seat

D. ▢ Move to the back of the bus to create space

**13. Which of the following is an example of a rail-based public transportation mode?**

A. ▢ Taxi

B. ▢ Bicycle-sharing program

C. ▢ Light rail

D. ▢ Carpool

**14. What does the term "farebox" refer to in public transportation?**

A. ▢ The driver's seat on a bus

B. ▢ The total number of passengers on a bus

C. ▢ The fare payment collection device on a bus

D. ▢ The designated waiting area for bus passengers

**15. True or False: Public transportation can help reduce traffic congestion and provide a more sustainable mode of transportation.**

A. ▢ True

B. ▢ False

# Correct answers for public transportation exam 3

**1. C** - To ensure priority for buses and reduce travel time

**2. False**

**3. D** - Convenient and faster fare payment

**4. D** - Bus

**5. D** - Avoiding paying the required fare

**6. C** - They help ensure orderly boarding and alighting of passengers

**7. C** - It requires vehicles to have a minimum number of occupants

**8. True**

**9. D** - To give buses priority at traffic signals for smoother flow

**10. B** - On the sidewalk or designated bus stop

**11. True**

**12. D** - Move to the back of the bus to create space

**13. C** - Light rail

**14. C** - The fare payment collection device on a bus

**15. True**

# Public transportation exam 4

### 1. Which of the following is a common mode of public transportation in urban areas?

A. ○ Taxis

B. ○ Limousines

C. ○ Car rentals

D. ○ Private helicopters

### 2. True or False: Public transportation systems are primarily funded through passenger fares and do not receive government subsidies.

A. ○ True

B. ○ False

### 3. What is the purpose of transit-oriented development (TOD)?

A. ○ To encourage private vehicle use

B. ○ To increase traffic congestion

C. ○ To promote mixed-use development near transit stations

D. ○ To reduce the number of public transportation options

### 4. Which of the following is an example of a paratransit service?

A. ○ Taxi

B. ○ Subway

C. ○ Ferry

D. ○ Light rail

**5. What is the purpose of a transfer ticket in public transportation?**

A. ▢ It allows unlimited travel for a specific duration

B. ▢ It provides discounts for future trips

C. ▢ It allows access to restricted areas

D. ▢ It allows for a seamless transfer between different routes or modes

**6. True or False: Public transportation is available 24/7 in all areas, including rural regions.**

A. ▢ True

B. ▢ False

**7. What is the primary function of a park-and-ride facility?**

A. ▢ To provide long-term parking for private vehicles

B. ▢ To accommodate large trucks and commercial vehicles

C. ▢ To offer recreational activities for public use

D. ▢ To facilitate the transfer from private vehicles to public transportation

**8. Which of the following is an advantage of using public transportation?**

A. ▢ Higher overall cost compared to private vehicles

B. ▢ Limited accessibility to specific locations

C. ▢ Reduced traffic congestion and environmental impact

D. ▢ Longer travel times due to frequent stops

**9. True or False: Public transportation is an inclusive mode of travel that caters to individuals with disabilities and special needs.**

A. ▢ True

B. ▢ False

**10. What does the term "headway" refer to in public transportation?**

A. ▢ The distance between bus stops

B. ▢ The speed limit for public transportation vehicles

C. ▢ The frequency of service or time between vehicles

D. ▢ The seating capacity of a public transportation vehicle

**11. How do bike-sharing programs contribute to public transportation?**

A. ▢ They provide free bicycles to commuters

B. ▢ They promote the use of private vehicles

C. ▢ They offer dedicated bike lanes on highways

D. ▢ They provide an additional mode of transportation for short distances

**12. True or False: Public transportation is an effective way to reduce carbon emissions and combat climate change.**

A. ▢ True

B. ▢ False

### 13. What is the purpose of a transit pass?

A. ▢ It grants unlimited access to public transportation for a specific period

B. ▢ It provides priority boarding for elderly passengers

C. ▢ It allows exclusive access to certain routes

D. ▢ It offers discounted fares for off-peak hours

### 14. Which of the following is a disadvantage of using public transportation?

A. ▢ Limited schedule and route options

B. ▢ Higher travel costs compared to private vehicles

C. ▢ Reduced safety and security measures

D. ▢ Unavailability of public transportation in rural areas

### 15. True or False: Public transportation systems aim to provide equal access and mobility options for all individuals, regardless of their socioeconomic status.

A. ▢ True

B. ▢ False

# Correct answers for public transportation exam 4

**1. A** - Taxis

**2. False**

**3. C** - To promote mixed-use development near transit stations

**4. A - Taxi**

**5. D** - It allows for a seamless transfer between different routes or modes

**6. False**

**7. D** - To facilitate the transfer from private vehicles to public transportation

**8. C** - Reduced traffic congestion and environmental impact

**9. True**

**10. C** - The frequency of service or time between vehicles

**11. D** - They provide an additional mode of transportation for short distances

**12. True**

**13. A** - It grants unlimited access to public transportation for a specific period

**14. A** - Limited schedule and route

# Public transportation exam 5

**1. What is the purpose of a transit signal priority (TSP) system?**

A. ○ To provide priority to public transportation vehicles at traffic signals

B. ○ To encourage private vehicle use during peak hours

C. ○ To reduce the frequency of public transportation services

D. ○ To increase traffic congestion in urban areas

**2. True or False: The use of electronic fare payment systems in public transportation has eliminated the need for physical tickets and passes.**

A. ○ True

B. ○ False

**3. What does the term "fare evasion" refer to in public transportation?**

A. ○ The act of paying a reduced fare for a longer trip

B. ○ The intentional failure to pay for a ticket or fare

C. ○ The process of transferring between different modes of transportation

D. ○ The act of purchasing multiple tickets for a single trip

**4. Which of the following is an example of demand-responsive transit?**

A. ○ Bus rapid transit (BRT)

B. ○ Light rail transit (LRT)

C. ○ Ridesharing services

D. ○ Commuter trains

**5. What is the purpose of a transit operator in public transportation?**

A. ▢ To provide customer service and assistance to passengers

B. ▢ To enforce fare payment regulations

C. ▢ To develop public transportation infrastructure

D. ▢ To operate private transportation services for corporate clients

**6. True or False: Public transportation agencies prioritize the convenience and comfort of passengers by offering amenities such as Wi-Fi and charging ports.**

A. ▢ True

B. ▢ False

**7. What is the purpose of a transit development plan?**

A. ▢ To establish a timeline for the construction of new transit stations

B. ▢ To identify areas of potential expansion for public transportation services

C. ▢ To promote the use of private vehicles over public transportation

D. ▢ To increase the fares for public transportation services

**8. Which of the following is an example of a fare collection method used in public transportation?**

A. ▢ Magnetic stripe cards

B. ▢ Paper tickets

C. ▢ Contactless smart cards

D. ▢ All of the above

**9. True or False: Public transportation systems aim to provide equal access and mobility options for all individuals, regardless of their socioeconomic status.**

A. ▢ True

B. ▢ False

**10. What is the purpose of a transit-oriented development (TOD)?**

A. ▢ To encourage private vehicle use near transit stations

B. ▢ To increase traffic congestion in urban areas

C. ▢ To promote mixed-use development near transit stations

D. ▢ To reduce the availability of public transportation options

**11. Which of the following is an advantage of using public transportation for commuting?**

A. ▢ Reduced travel time compared to private vehicles

B. ▢ Increased parking availability near workplaces

C. ▢ Lower overall cost compared to private vehicles

D. ▢ Limited accessibility to specific locations

**12. True or False: Public transportation systems prioritize the safety and security of passengers through measures such as surveillance cameras and emergency buttons.**

A. ▢ True

B. ▢ False

**13. What is the purpose of a transit app?**

A. ▢ To provide real-time information about public transportation schedules and routes

B. ▢ To offer exclusive discounts for public transportation fares

C. ▢ To allow passengers to request customized routes

D. ▢ To provide free Wi-Fi access on public transportation vehicles

**14. Which of the following is a disadvantage of using public transportation for daily commuting?**

A. ▢ Limited schedule and route options

B. ▢ Higher travel costs compared to private vehicles

C. ▢ Increased traffic congestion in urban areas

D. ▢ Higher parking fees near transit stations

**15. True or False: Public transportation systems play a crucial role in reducing traffic congestion and air pollution in urban areas.**

A. ▢ True

B. ▢ False

# Correct answers for public transportation exam 5

**1. A** - To provide priority to public transportation vehicles at traffic signals

**2. True**

**3. B -** The intentional failure to pay for a ticket or fare

**4. C** - Ridesharing services

**5. A** - To provide customer service and assistance to passengers

**6. True**

**7. B** - To identify areas of potential expansion for public transportation services

**8. D** - All of the above

**9. True**

**10. C** - To promote mixed-use development near transit stations

**11. C** - Lower overall cost compared to private vehicles

**12. True**

**13. A** - To provide real-time information about public transportation schedules and routes

**14. A** - Limited schedule and route options

**15. True**

# Conclusion

Congratulations on reaching the end of the Minnesota DMV Exam Workbook! This comprehensive guide has provided you with the necessary knowledge and skills to navigate the roads of the Land of 10,000 Lakes safely, responsibly, and in compliance with the state's driving laws and regulations. Throughout this book, we have covered a wide range of topics, including traffic laws and signs, vehicle control and safety, alcohol and drugs, vehicle equipment and maintenance, sharing the road, transportation of hazardous materials, vehicle registration and insurance, emergencies, vehicle size and weight limits, and public transportation.

By studying and understanding these chapters, you have acquired the foundational knowledge needed to become a skilled and responsible driver. You now possess a deeper understanding of the traffic laws and signs that govern our roadways, the importance of vehicle control and safety measures, the risks associated with alcohol and drugs, the significance of proper vehicle maintenance, the principles of sharing the road with others, the precautions necessary when transporting hazardous materials, the requirements for vehicle registration and insurance, the preparedness needed for emergencies, the considerations of vehicle size and weight limits, and the advantages of utilizing public transportation.

Remember, the journey to becoming a safe and responsible driver does not end with this book. It is crucial to continually educate yourself, stay updated on new laws and regulations, and practice safe driving habits. Strive to be a lifelong learner, as the driving landscape is constantly evolving, and it is essential to adapt to new challenges and technologies.

As you prepare for your Minnesota DMV exam, take the time to review and reinforce the information presented in this workbook. Test your knowledge by utilizing the practice questions and scenarios provided throughout each chapter. Consider enrolling in additional driver education courses or seeking guidance from experienced drivers or driving instructors to further enhance your skills.

Always prioritize safety and responsibility when operating a vehicle. Remember to buckle up, obey traffic laws, respect other road users, and avoid distractions while driving. Be mindful of the potential consequences of reckless behavior and the impact it can have on yourself and others.

Lastly, we would like to express our gratitude for your commitment to safe driving. By taking the initiative to study and prepare for your Minnesota DMV exam, you have demonstrated a commendable dedication to becoming a responsible driver. Your efforts contribute to creating a safer and more harmonious driving environment for all residents of Minnesota.

As you embark on your driving journey, always remember that safety is everyone's responsibility. Each time you get behind the wheel, make a conscious effort to prioritize the safety of yourself, your passengers, and fellow road users. By adhering to the knowledge and principles presented in this workbook, you are well on your way to becoming a confident and responsible driver on Minnesota's roads.

Best wishes for success on your Minnesota DMV exam and in your future endeavors as a skilled and responsible driver. Drive safely and enjoy the journey!

Made in the USA
Monee, IL
05 September 2024

65152434R00162